E.D.I.N.A.:

Energy Medicine from the Stars!

Shamanism for the 21ˢᵗ Century and Beyond

By Lois J. Wetzel, MFA

E.D.I.N.A.:

Energy Medicine from the Stars!

Shamanism for the 21st Century and Beyond

By Lois J. Wetzel, MFA

Copyright 2012

Publisher: Hot Pink Lotus POD

Houston, Texas

Front Cover Design & Image: Lathan at Oneness Pixels

Acknowledgements

I acknowledge and appreciate the clients who let me experiment in the beginning with using an untried modality which no one had ever heard of upon them, and who paid careful attention to how using E.D.I.N.A. affected them after they left the healing room—and reported that back to me. This appreciation especially includes my first female client, Dana Tibbs, and my first male client, David Germain, upon whom E.D.I.N.A. was first practiced.

Gratitude is also extended to the students from all over the Earth who have been guided to be initiated into E.D.I.N.A. and answered that call. They have used it to heal and balance family, friends, pets and even their clients. A big hug goes out to those who have written about it on their websites, building the internet presence for E.D.I.N.A. And I especially thank all of the E.D.I.N.A. Instructors, past, present and future whose efforts continue to spread the miracle that is E.D.I.N.A. across the globe.

A deep honor belongs to the E.D.I.N.A. FIRST HUNDRED INITIATES who helped ground this energy into the planet, thereby making the energy stronger. This increased the morphogenetic field of E.D.I.N.A. to the point that it became clear the method would survive. They did this, and still do it, simply by allowing the energy to run through their bodies—whether or not they actually practice E.D.I.N.A. regularly. By carrying this frequency, they are ensuring the spiritual evolution of humanity. Those who practice E.D.I.N.A. regularly make the morphogenetic field of E.D.I.N.A. even stronger still, as do the all people who become initiated—simply by carrying this frequency in their bodies and energy fields. Their participation increases the force field of the healing energy for everyone who does E.D.I.N.A.! The more of us there are the larger the energetic field of E.D.I.N.A. on Earth from which we all can draw.

Table of Contents

Introduction

As of this writing, early 2012, there is much talk about when and if "extra-terrestrials" will make themselves known to humanity. This is expected to happen soon, and notions about what that will look like abound. Some posit that spaceships will land on the White House lawn. This does not take into account that many highly advanced beings do not need machines to travel through spacetime, though some do. I am here to tell you about how a few of the beings which do not need machines are already showing up in our world, and have been so doing for a very long time. This is not occurring in the manner most people imagine this could or would happen.

As we expand and increase our frequency of vibration, we will begin to more easily and more often perceive the expanded realms in which these advanced beings exist. Beings from Sirius-B have been appearing to me for a very long time, and I have been working with them in the healing setting. They have appeared to others as well, including but not limited to my students. These beings are blue in color; perhaps you have seen them as well. They have come to me to teach a form of energy medicine for ascension. They first came to work with me for a couple of years in about 1998 and left for a few years telling me they would be back later. They returned five years later telling me to take dictation for a new form of energy medicine. That is what this book is about.

As I begin this project, I do wonder if I can remember it all. Of course, now I realize I should have been keeping a journal the whole time. I kept having that thought, but did not follow through. Or when I did keep a journal, it was about personal items of interest only to me, not metaphysical or spiritual occurrences in my life that were a lot more inter-esting, rare and special than the personal encounters after my divorce. By now I know that when I am having these thoughts pop into my head like, "You should really be keep-ing a journal," it's not me thinking it, but someone else say-ing it, someone I cannot yet see. I realize that most people have not come to this conclusion, but I am aware that there very few original thoughts. Instead, there are Guides, or An-gels, or extra-dimensional beings of different kinds around us all the time saying things to us. We just tell ourselves these are our thoughts. Often these beings are giving us ex-traordinary ideas! This isn't new, either. It has always been the case. One of the greatest inventors of the 20th Century, Nikola Tesla, was aware of this phenomenon. He told a few people that his inventions and ideas came from beings from Sirius. I only quite recently learned this about Tesla years after I began taking dictation from them and working with them in the healing setting. Imagine my shock!

Years ago, when these particular beings from Sirius came to me and began talking to me, I thought I was the only person in the world to whom anything like this had ever happened. They were not identifying themselves as angels or anything Biblical like that, but as Starbeings from Sirius-B. That was so outlandish that initially I thought it most likely was just my imagination. It wasn't until they began to tell me things I absolutely did not and could not already know about, and then sending confirmation to me out in the world from some other source, that I began to realize they were real. I could not see them with my eyes open, you see.

They tell me this is because their frequency is different than ours, so they are in a different dimension as we would say. Actually, they tell me the better word is "density" not dimen-sion. They try to explain this to me, but we do not have the words in our world yet. The sense I get is that their molecules vibrate faster than ours and this is what sends them into a different frequency or density. They keep giving me the metaphoric image of lightweight things floating upward in water. Denser things are down at the bottom of the ocean. As they/we become lighter, as the molecules vibrate ever faster, we float upward a bit higher. When they have become light enough, they float up out of the water and up into the air, which is a very different density than the water. If they want to get down to the bottom of the water so we dense ones can see them they have to become dense again, and it is quite unpleasant to them. They do not mean to be rude, but this is just the truth. It is out of extreme love that a Starbeing would do such a thing for us, even temporarily. They say that this density explanation is not complete, but is the best they can do given our scientific knowledge at this point in time.

These beings are completely made of light, but they were once dense at the bottom of the ocean like we. They give assurances that if we keep on evolving spiritually, we will be made of light someday, too. They are here to midwife that process.

This is why they came to me when they did. It's this process of turning ourselves into light which is called ascension. They came to bring in a method of healing and balancing and releasing detritus which makes it easier for us to ascend. These highly evolved beings want to help us. They have asked me to tell people about it and teach them how to do it. I often wished aloud they would find someone else to do it, but they did not. So here I am, doing as they have asked.

As I explained on my E.D.I.N.A. website—starting several years ago—there are definite symptoms of ascension. These symptoms can make a person feel really awful at times. That *is why these beings came to help us—so it would not be so difficult or painful. They have been through this before and they know what it is like. When we resist the ascension process, and when we cannot find a way to get rid of our gunk, detritus, pathogenic energy and be rebalanced, we can feel truly horrible.*

I am going to tell you the story of how they initially came to me and worked with me in the healing room and taught me. I will tell you how I began to share this with others and teach others how to work with these Starbeings. Then I am going to tell you how you can work with them, too.

Chapter 1
The Background

Those brave enough to incarnate at this time in history are witnessing an unprecedented, miraculous time on earth. When we made the decision to come here, the outcome was not at all clear. All of us knew we were taking a great risk being born during this period, but the potential for enormous spiritual rewards and profound joy were so great we all stood in line to be here at this time.

As our Souls had hoped, we are expanding into much greater versions of ourselves. Because of this, we are beginning to be aware of many things which have always coexisted simultaneously with us, but which we were unable to perceive while in physical form. An example of this are the Light Beings which are always present, such as angels and other extra-dimensional beings. As we ascend and expand our perceptions, we are more easily making contact with these kinds of life forms, or finally becoming aware of them. Sometimes this happens with our eyes open, other times with our eyes closed. Many of us receive telepathic communication from them if we allow ourselves to do so. Most of them are here because they desire to help us as we are being birthed into expanded and more conscious versions of ourselves.

The problem with receiving this kind of help is that the vast majority of us have been told since we were small that our psychic perception was "just imagination." So even when these beings successfully make themselves heard or seen in our mind's eye, we ignore them or brush them off as not real—as imaginary. We do this as if our imagination were not the supremely fine and exquisitely beautiful trait that it is.

I can say without equivocation that our imagination is almost totally the same thing as our psychic perceptions. If you are one of the fortunate ones who can close his/her eyes and see visual images in your mind's eye, or a movie playing in your head, you are clairvoyant. If you hear beings speaking to you inside your head, you are clairaudient. If you have a felt sense of things unknowable, yet you know them, you are clairsentient. The belief that this makes you a crazy person is mistaken.

There are those who are alarmed at the concept of "hearing voices." The only time to be worried about "hearing voices" is if the voices are saying bad things about you or someone else, or if they are telling you to harm yourself or others. This is when medical attention is warranted. This information comes from the American Psychiatric Association's Diagnostic and Statistical Manual. This is the reference manual psychologists and psychiatrists use to diagnose mental illness. The book does not, however, refer to the other voices when diagnosing schizophrenia. By other voices I mean those not saying bad things, those who speak to mystics, psychics, intuitives and mediums. Spirit Guides and angels, for example, do not say negative or scary things. If we are smart, though, we do not usually tell just anyone about seeing or hearing or otherwise sensing these "things that are not there." If your family does not have an admitted or known history of psychics, mediums or mystics, you may have had these abilities all along, and not have had any guidance at all about this subject. The people in need of medical help are those who not only hear voices saying bad things, but who additionally often expect everyone else to see and hear things not part of "ordinary reality." Adults should be able to distinguish between ordinary reality and that which others cannot normally perceive.

Yet as we continue to expand, greater numbers of us will be seeing things in our heads and hearing voices, feeling touches with no discernible source, smelling things and having odd tastes in our mouths, which are "psychic" in nature. Of course, eventually one day everyone will have these abilities. So our definition of reality will be rapidly evolving.

My own family did not have a known or admitted history of psychics or mediums, and it is some kind of miracle that I have allowed myself as an adult to turn my abilities back on. I suspect Birdie Leona Moore, my Irish immigrant great-grandmother who died of Swine Flu in 1918 at the age of thirty-seven was probably the one who carried the genes. I know my mother is incredibly psychic, but will not admit it. She knows things she has no other way to know. Many people of her generation have thought they were insane if they had psychic abilities. Sadly, this is what has happened to many of the gifted psychic/intuitive people in western civilization. Many are medicated or hospitalized in hopes of making them "normal" again. This is a tremendous loss to us as a race of beings, for these people's insights are essential to having a well-rounded civilization.

I also saw and heard things that "were not there" quite well as a child, but this upset the adults, especially my mother. In fact, it upset her to the point that I just totally shut myself down—at least as much as I could. I have an ongoing habit of ignoring a lot of what I perceive intuitively as a result of that early coping mechanism.

Over a period of more than twenty-five years of seriously pursuing enlightenment and meditating for over thirty-five years, I have at last reached a place where I allow most of that kind of communication to come through. It is through just such communication with extra-dimensional beings from Sirius-B called The Ankenash that E.D.I.N.A. energy medicine came to Earth via a very reluctant me.

So since at this point the reader is probably wondering, "What is E.D.I.N.A.?" I will tell you. E.D.I.N.A. is an acronym that stands for Energy Dynamics for the Integration of Natural Attributes. This is a form of energy medicine which works directly upon the human Light Body, which each of us possess. We each have an energetic duplicate of our physical body right down to the smallest organelle in each cell and it is called the Light Body. Among the several "natural attributes" which need integrating in the modern human are our expanded sensory abilities; clairvoyance, clairaudience, clairsentience and so on. But there is more. Our auric fields are expanding and our relationship to the magnetic grid of the Earth is changing. For this reason we can develop through no fault or error of our own, cracks and fissures in our auras affecting our Light Bodies. These need to be healed or repaired. E.D.I.N.A. does this type of healing, among other things. It can and does also heal us spiritually, emotionally, mentally and physically.

And what is meant by energy medicine? The term "energy medicine" also includes such healing modalities as Reiki, Touch for Health, Quantum Healing, Psych-K, BodyTalk System, Quantum Touch, Theta Healing, and Matrix Energetics to name a few. With energy medicine, a natural healing response is triggered by the manipulation of subtle energies. But E.D.I.N.A. is different than the others because it directly works on the human Light Body first. Healing by working on the Light Body is nothing new; actually it is ancient. Shamanic practitioners all over the planet used similar Light Body healing techniques eons ago, though these methods have been largely lost over the ages. Changes to the Light Body will affect the physical, emotional and spiritual levels of the individual. While most of us cannot see the Light Body, we definitely can feel it. When we practice E.D.I.N.A., almost everyone can feel the light as it is introduced into various parts of the body. E.D.I.N.A. helps with the ascension process, to make the process more efficient and more comfortable for us. This technique also gradually reconnects the 12-strand DNA due to the efforts of The Ankenash in the expanded realms. A fully functioning 12-strand DNA is our birthright as Light Beings on earth.

Perhaps you are wondering what a Light Body is. Some call the Light Body the energy body. It is the energetic duplicate, right down to the cellular level, of our physical body. This is what leaves as we die. It has mass. If an adult person is on a hospital scale when they die, it is reported that they lose between eight and thirteen ounces at the moment of death. This clearly indicates that the Soul has mass! A light also leaves the human body at the moment of death. I personally saw this phenomenon of light leaving three distinct times while giving a stranger CPR in an airport in 1990. The light left his body and returned and left again three times as I gave CPR to an elderly man who had collapsed in the airport. I could clearly see the skin glow and the eyes sparkle when he was in his body. Each time he left the body it looked flat and vacant, like an object, not a body. The eyes were dull and flat. When he returned his skin glowed immediately and his eyes sparkled until he left the body again.

Clear evidence of the Light Body also comes to us in the form of Kirlian photography where the Light Body makes an imprint on the film. Light can be photographed coming out of the hands of healers. If you use that photographic technique to look at a leaf, you will see a glowing version of the leaf. Then tear off a piece of the leaf, and you will still see light coming from the entire leaf in the next photo you take. Why? It's because the leaf's Light Body remains whole. And if a person has an arm or leg amputated, we know that they will still have sensations in the missing limb. It may ache or itch, for example. This is called "phantom limb" syndrome. The person is actually feeling these sensations in the Light Body of the missing arm or leg. The Light Body can feel things!

And so in E.D.I.N.A. we work with the Light Body directly in our healing sessions. We introduce etheric light into the person, precise colors are required at specific locations. Following a protocol, we connect to the E.D.I.N.A. energies and follow instructions from The Ankenash, the Starbebeings from Sirius-B, who work with us with permission of Earth's Spiritual Heirarchy (our Spiritual Hierarchy includes the angels, Archangels, Archoi, The Ascended Masters, Jesus, Buddha, Mohammed, Kwan Yin, St. Germain, Hilarion, etc.). After we invoke them, The Ankenash instruct us as to which techniques from the E.D.I.N.A. cache to utilize for each particular client, and in what sequence. No two sessions are exactly alike since no two clients are the same. The Ankenash work on our clients (or ourselves) in the expanded realms at the same time we are working in the three/ four dimensions (or densities). Communicating with us telepathically either by words heard clairaudiently, or visions of what to do next, or just a felt sense, these Starbeings generously assist and guide us in the healing session. This etheric light/energy also comes out through the palms of the initiates hands, in a fashion similar to Reiki. In the advanced E.D.I.N.A. classes we learn to additionally connect to the fifth dimensional ascended beings called the Hathors for assistance with our sound healing techniques. The human voice is the most powerful sound healing tool we have!

We also use tuning forks and Tibetan or crystal bowls. Vocal toning is not required, especially not for those who are not comfortable with vocal toning.

As has been said, E.D.I.N.A. can be used on yourself or upon others. There is a very simple initial class called Basic E.D.I.N.A. which I will relate in detail in this book so you can do this work as well—if you choose. This is the class which has provided the initiation which allows the healer to connect to The Ankenash in the healing setting. This initiation can be done in person or at a distance. Gradually more techniques are being given to us from these Starbeings of Sirius-B, and then shared in advanced classes, which are numbered modules, for those who are interested in learning more. Energetic light, color, sound, sacred geometry and more are used, including some medical chi gong and shamanic techniques. Numerous methods that were lost after the High Period of Atlantis are being reassembled in this form of healing—the parts having been fragmented and spread about all over the planet and pieces retained in various cultures. In the advanced modules, there are techniques which have been given to me, E.D.I.N.A.'s founder, Lois Wetzel, which do not exist anywhere else on Earth, as they had been lost completely. And some are new techniques altogether.

What have we seen healed with E.D.I.N.A.? Well, snoring for one. Don't laugh. It can be really important in a marriage to be able to sleep with the beloved! Some of the other reports include noticeable emotional healing in groups of prison inmates, relief from or positive changes in the symptoms of narcolepsy, reversal of hearing loss, emotional disorders, insomnia, panic disorders, allergies, back pain, digestive problems, terminal blood diseases, diabetes and joint pain just to name a few. Post-traumatic stress which people experience after violent trauma such as combat or rape can be relieved. Nightmares in children, pain from nerve damage, headaches, nervousness, depression, tumors have been seen to improve or go away after sufficient E.D.I.N.A. sessions. There seems to be no limit to what E.D.I.N.A. can heal as we continue to experiment with this new technique—new to humans, at least, but of course not to The Ankenash who have worked with humans at many points in history over hundreds of thousands of years on Earth. They are introducing a new level of healing frequencies at this time because humans are finally ready, having increased their vibrational frequencies beyond what anyone in the expanded realms thought possible a mere thirty years ago!

Here are examples of healings reported by E.D.I.N.A. Initiates:

A woman who worked with prison inmates' emotional issues had been using Ho'oponopono until she found E.D.I.N.A. She then began to do them both at the same time: Ho'oponopono with the E.D.I.N.A. portal open. From this woman comes this:

"Lois, I use EDINA energies as an overlay for every meditation and exercise I ever do now. The healing and growth is absolutely incredible, compared to not using it...

As a follow up to the projects I did with the inmates last year, this time I used Ho'oponopono without the EDINA overlay on each offender, just on myself. I did this to test for results. I will never do that again. The results are measurably greater when I use the EDINA energy connection on behalf of each inmate individually."
~ J.B. Houston, Texas

And from a woman in Beaumont, Texas:

"I did an E.D.I.N.A. treatment on a lady who had a stroke a few months ago. Her left hand and arm have been paralyzed ever since her stroke. I worked on her Sunday, and she went to physical therapy the next day. That day for the first time she was able to move the arm. It was the first time she could do that since she had her stroke. The therapist was amazed. The client said she could feel the energy in her arm during the treatment—I was really running hot. It was almost painfully intense for me as the healing energy moved through me to her. She can move her arm backward now from the shoulder on her own—again, for the first time since her stroke. She was so excited! Me, too! I had done a presentation on E.D.I.N.A. at our Body, Mind Spirit group last week. It was after hearing my talk that she asked me to do a treatment for her—so I did.

Thank you so much, Lois, for sharing this wonderful healing modality with me and the world."
~ Candy M., College Professor

And another E.D.I.N.A. initiate reported about her experience working with a client who'd had a stroke:

"Thanks for sharing, Candy, about your experience with the person who had a stroke. I also did a treatment with E.D.I.N.A. on my mother after her stroke as she was dizzy. As soon as I did the treatment the dizziness went away and has never come back. I do not have any clients professionally, but work on my family and my dog. I have had such good success with this, and I hope to be able to start doing it more when I retire and do not have a full time job."
~ Glenna R., Business Owner in Florida

Francine, who has been practicing energy medicine for

years, BodyTalk, Reiki and Psych-K, reports right after getting her Basic E.D.I.N.A. energy medicine initiation:

"There were more 'beings' present in the healing room after my Basic E.D.I.N.A. initiation. I am seeing greater details in my sessions, and the sessions are much more fluid. I need to do fewer sessions to get faster and better results. I have been seeing this in clients who had been seeing other energy healers. They come to me and I use E.D.I.N.A. and they get better faster. Right after my Basic E.D.I.N.A. class, I began to draw more new clients, and they are more 'evolved' clients, it seems to me, more spiritual types."

Laura, a school teacher, reports this:

"I was actually thinking about you and E.D.I.N.A. today, remembering my class and initiation. I wanted to let you know that shortly after my initiation last year, I started right away to use the E.D.I.N.A. energy medicine on a friend of mine who had just been diagnosed with breast cancer. The cancer had spread to her blood and bones, and the docs were not giving her much longer to live—five years at the most. I started E.D.I.N.A. treatments along with Reiki in January and by the following May, they said that she had a complete remission of her cancer. It was gone. I do not know how that happened, but I would like to think that the Reiki and E.D.I.N.A. treatments helped with that, but I still wonder."

In the following example we can see how the effects of E.D.I.N.A. can actually be seen on the hospital monitors. Carol, an advanced E.D.I.N.A. initiate in Dallas, Texas, had a powerful experience in which she was called to the hospital room of an old friend who had been in a severe motorcycle accident. The patient's wife had called Carol to come to the hospital and "lay her healing hands on him." Jon was in the ICU unconscious and rigged up to machines.

Carol's rather skeptical husband came in, too. As Carol put her hands on Jon and connected to the E.D.I.N.A. energies, everyone could see the patient's monitors change immediately to indicate a more healthy, relaxed state. At one point Carol's husband put his hand on Jon and the other hand on Carol's back, and felt the E.D.I.N.A. energy arc through his body to Jon. He jumped and looked startled, giving her a wide-eyed look, but kept his hands there. *Her husband's attitude toward her and her work has shifted dramatically in a very positive way since then, much to her delight.*

Jon, and especially his wife who was actually conscious and alert when all this was going on, credit Carol's E.D.I.N.A. work with his fast recovery, the speed of which had his doctors completely baffled.

Mieko in Japan has reported that her son had an asthma attack at school and she rushed to her small child's side. When she got there she began doing E.D.I.N.A. on him and the attack was over within five minutes, when usually they lasted far longer.

Cynthia reports that to her great upset and dismay two of her usual energy medicine clients developed cancer symptoms at the same time. She had been practicing another modality and then learned E.D.I.N.A. She states:

"After the first EDINA session, the first client, who has survived two bouts of breast cancer/chemo/radiation, felt exhausted and awful. She had been told when she received her last chemo round two years earlier, that she had got the maximum lifetime dose and could not have more should the cancer come back. The woman had also been warned that leukemia was a possibility down the road. When she developed broken capillaries on the trunk of her body, she went to her oncologist who is also a close friend. The doctor

cried at the appointment; she was sure that this was leukemia and thought the patient did not have long to live.

I shared an office with the ailing client at the time, and she came to me and told me that she most likely had leukemia and would be closing the practice. We did another session with EDINA and Body Chemistry details. She reported that after the session she felt The Ankenash wake her up at night and work on her since she had already given permission for them to be involved in her healing. When she next got her blood work from the next doctor's appointment, the abnormal leukemia cells were present in her blood and bone marrow, but the doctor was perplexed because they were not multiplying at the expected rate of speed. A week after the first blood test, the new tests indicated that the leukemia cells were 80 percent cleared. A month later, the leukemia cells were undetectable. The client now says she feels better than she has felt in ten years.

The second woman had uterine and ovarian cancer and had a hysterectomy a few years ago at a very young age, as she is now only twenty-eight years of age. She had been told she had HPV virus, which is sometimes associated with cervical cancer, and had other issues associated with HPV. After her first E.D.I.N.A. session she started having symptoms which pointed to cervical cancer. Upon doing a vaginal exam, her doc warned her that cervical cancer was what it looked like. He chose to do an advanced pap smear stat and made the appointment for a biopsy. She also received her results after her second session with EDINA and Body Chemistry details, plus she reported feeling The Ankenash working on her at odd times. Her doctor was perplexed and pleased the next time he saw her. Not only was the disturbance he had seen gone, but her pap smear was completely normal. She was shocked. She had NEVER before had a normal pap smear.

Not only this, but the HPV was undetectable. She was abso-lutely ecstatic.

I have to admit, this whole process was quite scary for me. I took it personally that two people I had been working on for quite a while using BodyTalk had cancer scares at the same time. I could not understand why they had this coming on, or in their bodies, and it was not addressed in a way that I could recognize that was what we were working on.

I could not prove why this healing result happened, but I am very happy that both clients are healthy now.

Certainly this EDINA energy medicine is interesting stuff, that's for sure! ~ Cynthia, Basic EDINA Initiate

Lois' Note: It is not uncommon for The Ankenash to work on people outside the treatment room once they have been given permission to work with us. Our clients often see them in hospital rooms as well—some call them 'blue angels'. As for the use of more than one modality in Cynthia's situation with her clients as above mentioned, it is common for people to be worked on with more than one modality at a time, including the ministrations of medical doctors alongside one or more forms of energy medicine, and/or with supplements, herbs, acupuncture and so on. It is impossible to tease apart what modality healed what, in fact, they have probably worked in concert. Only human curiosity or perhaps occasionally the healer's ego even demands to know. For the healed client, the healing experience is all that matters. And so it should be!

The college professor in Beaumont, Candy, also reported that she worked on a seriously ill feline which had diabetes in addition to her multiple other health issues. After a couple of treatments, the cat had an insulin crisis, needing more than usual for a short while, and then the needs for meds backed way down. She then required a different type of insulin altogether, but in a vastly smaller dose. The cat died of kidney failure a few months later, so Candy never learned if the cat could be completely healed of diabetes or not. With energy medicine it is not uncommon to have people experience a healing curve where they require more meds briefly, and then level off to requiring much less than before the session.

One Instructor and Advanced E.D.I.N.A. Initiate, David Germain, sent far more lengthy reports of two healing experiences. One is with a home health-care nurse, Susan, and one is a healing experience with an elderly patient of hers, Lee Roy. In Susan's report which follows, she mentions having been in a strange state of sleep while David was working on her. This was her first experience with any kind of energy medicine at all, and frequently people will describe going into a light trance as being "asleep." I believe this is what happened with Susan. Clients frequently go into a light trance state while receiving energy medicine. Also she mentions three days of discomfort, which can happen when a profound healing experience occurs, especially if a person has never had energy medicine before. Such discomfort is quite rare, but possible.

The following is a letter from E.D.I.N.A. Instructor, Practitioner and Houston area shaman David Germain about these healing experiences, written in early February of 2012:

Dear Lois,

Susie Brown is an experienced nurse in her late forties who first contacted me to work on her bedridden patient. She suffered severe back pain from the daily strain of struggling to move him. For her session, I asked her to stretch out on the couch, lying on her stomach. I put on a CD of therapeutic music, cleared the space, and opened the EDINA portal. The entire session lasted 45 minutes and focused on her lower back. I drew light into her second chakra and sent energy until I actually felt her spine move and realign beneath my hands. Not only did she experience relief of the pain, but a huge release of what I feel must have been Kundalini energy that lasted for three days.

The following are Nurse Brown's unedited comments about her experience receiving her first treatment with EDINA Energy Medicine.

"I am writing to tell of my experience after receiving my first session with EDINA energy work. I am a nurse by profession and was used to traditional methods of medicine and healing so when I chose to have this type of energy work performed on me, it was quite different. I chose to have energy work done on me mainly because of the help I saw it gave with a friend/patient of mine at the time. It helped my friend/patient so much to the point to where I wanted to see if it would have the same positive effects on me.

I received my first session in the summer of 2011. I have a lower back injury that was sustained years ago, and the prescribed medicine I had still left me with a nagging pain, so I asked David if he would do some energy work on me, and he did. My first session was amazing to say the least. I can remember David telling me to just relax, and I did. I fell sound asleep, but it was a different kind of sleep. I was somewhere else, a good place. I actually felt a shifting in my lower back as I slept; I felt my bones moving.

I remember David awakening me after the session was over.

He asked me how I felt. I felt great and all of the nagging

pain in my back that was seemingly always there was gone, but what was more unexplainable to me was how I felt for the three days after my first session.

I became restless, agitated with the feeling of wanting to be in seclusion. I tried to disguise these feelings but could not. I had a loss of appetite, did not want to be around anyone at all! I did not want to see the sun, or man made light I actually stayed to myself, with little or no conversation with my husband or dogs. I would not answer my phone. I felt scared, but I did not know what I was scared of. I even said to myself, "What have I let be done to me? My God I never felt so, so, helpless!"

I also remember I had an unusual thirst for nothing but water, I lived on vitamin supplements and water for three days, and the only thing I thought was good was that the nagging ache was gone from my back. I had very little sleep for three days, but I was not tired, just the opposite, I was fully charged up wondering what was happening to me?

I lay in bed the third night staring at the ceiling thinking for the love of God, what did I get myself into. I finally fell asleep that third night, and when I opened my eyes the fourth day I felt Magnificent! Wonderful! Happy! I jumped up and it was a beautiful sunny day! My husband ran upstairs because he heard me crying and laughing at the same time, and he said honey what's wrong? I told him, nothing is wrong. I feel great! And I did feel great!!! During my three days of feeling just the opposite, David kept in close touch with me, but I was so thrilled with joy to let him know what the fourth day brought: sheer joy and happiness.

I refer to those three days as my three days in limbo (smiles) but the fourth day, felt as if I was shot out of cannon straight from limbo, and right onto the path of a new awakening, a new sense of peace and happiness! It was a sensation I will never forget for as long as I live.

Needless to say I am now a regular client, and I still get so much of a great feeling out of all my EDINA therapy sessions with David. I am amazed at how it has helped me with other areas of my life.

I know that there are skeptics who would question energy work, and that is their right! But as for me, especially being in the health field myself, I have never experienced such an awakening as I have had with this EDINA energy work. I thought I had just about seen it all, but I was wrong, and that is okay, because now I now know that there is more than just traditional medicine. I am blessed and humbled at the experience, and speaking for myself as a nurse, if I had the authority, I would make EDINA energy work mandatory for all of those who are in need of relief from any kind of pain. If it works for me, it surely can work for all.

With Deep Fondness & Appreciation,
Susie M. Brown R.N., BSN

As mentioned before, Nurse Brown additionally had a bed-ridden patient, Lee Roy, for whom David did several sessions spread out over a period of time before he worked on Susie. David's descriptions of these sessions with Lee Roy are detailed below. Along with these are two letters from Nurse Brown. David states:

"Lee Roy was my EDINA client from March, 2011 until his death the following September. He was 85 years old. His condition at the time was diagnosed as "Congestive Heart Failure." He had survived multiple heart attacks and wore a pacemaker.

When I first saw him he was completely bed-ridden. He had the most severe muscle spasms I have ever seen, his body almost completely rigid, and had a great deal of trouble speaking clearly. After his first EDINA session, I received the following letter from his live-in nurse, Susan Brown:

David,

It is simply incredible too see such a change in Lee Roy, only after only one session! He is very happy! He cannot believe that he is actually feeling so good, that he has 'not felt this good in a long time' are his own words. Family and friends have been calling to see how his session went and Lee Roy is telling them all, that he feels that this EDINA energy therapy is what he needs. Lee Roy really is hopeful that more sessions will benefit him even more!

Lee Roy's two sons even called to see how his therapy session went and they are truly amazed. I spoke with them both afterwards and they said that their Dad had spoken to them with such clarity, not stuttering or stammering as he usually does when they talk with him.

THANKS a million, David!!!!!!

Peace& Light...Susie

Then David continues...

"During Lee Roy's second EDINA session four days later, I sensed a strong flow of energy, and I was guided intuitively that he needed he needed to be detoxified with a combination of energy work and a special bath. Afterwards, I instructed his nurse to give him an apple cider vinegar bath and lots of water to drink.

Because it was already quite late, his nurse waited to bathe him in the morning. When his doctor visited Lee Roy later that day, the water was still in the tub, and he observed its unusual dark color. He took samples for testing and reported that it contained a strong concentration of heavy metals and many residual chemicals that occurred from the breakdown of Lee Roy's prescription medications. At the time Lee Roy was taking a variety of medications including: prescriptions for muscle relaxants, cholesterol lowering agent, blood pressure lowering medication and a blood thinner.

I continued to work on this elderly patient twice a week over the coming months and soon his cholesterol and blood pressure tested within normal ranges. Eventually he was taken off all medications by his doctor as a result of the energy work he received from me.

On several occasions, I did EDINA sessions with Lee Roy, just prior to his bi-weekly physical therapy. The results were nothing short of remarkable. His therapist was stunned by his increased muscle control which enabled him to stand with less assistance and for a longer duration than during any previous physical therapy sessions.

But the most noticeable change in was his overall personality and demeanor.

Lee Roy, you see, was a decorated World War II veteran, and he had seen many atrocities and terrible suffering during his service. Now years later, his wartime experience combined with his ill health and confinement had made him a deeply bitter man. He cursed and swore at his family and abused his nurse. He was miserable, and often spoke of wanting to die. He saw many psychiatrists and psychologists but none of them seemed to help and were eventually dismissed.

Soon after first receiving EDINA, Lee Roy's attitude began to change, and his outlook dramatically improved. His friends commented that he was more like his old self, and he seemed take pleasure in life again. It was as if you could see his ascension taking place. When he did eventually pass on, it was with a great sense of peace and tranquility.

After he passed, I received phone calls of gratitude from both of his sons and the following letter from his nurse:

David,

I am writing you to give you my perception of the experience Lee Roy had from you doing the EDINA energy work on him the many times that you did. I knew it would not keep him from dying, but you prolonged his life a bit longer because you gave him what all of the doctors he had could not give him, and they really tried! You gave him something he had been searching for: PEACE, TRANQUILITY, ACCEPTANCE and faith...all of which he had heard about, but he never had the chance to live it until you worked on him.

I can tell you this for sure, that before you took him on as a client and I was caring for him for more than 10 years, Lee Roy had never been more at peace! Peaceful moments, yes, but no true, lasting peace until your energy work began. He had a lot of hurt and bitterness in him, mainly due to his time in the service to his country, seeing hurtful conditions no one should ever have to see or to live.

He carried the hurt for many years, has seen lots of psychiatrists psychologists, etc. to help him find some peace. He was prescribed many medications to help him deal with his depression, but they were eventually discontinued because they did not help him at all. In fact the meds made it worse. It was not until you started to treat him that I and all who knew him saw a change for the better. He used to wake up every day and curse the day because he was alive to see it. When I asked if you would see him as a client, Lee Roy was confused as how your kind of medicine could ever help him, because with your energy therapy there was no physical pill to swallow.

I recall after the first session, Lee Roy had smiled because he said that your "magic" made him feel better. He was still unsure of how you did it, but it made him feel better, so he agreed to another session. I remember that after you did a detoxification on him, WOW! After releasing his beast inside if you will...he was a whole new person, he was visibly happier and very congenial with me especially. He would even tell me that he loved me very, very much! I knew he did love me, but Lee Roy was the type of person who felt telling someone he loved them was a sign of weakness, but he actually was saying it all the time especially after his detox. I can truthfully say that after the detoxification he lost all the hurt and gained all the love. He was at peace with his condition, he smiled, which was very rare before. He woke every day and smiled when it was sun, rain or clouds.

He used to tell his friends when talking with them that 'Mr. Magic is coming this evening' to fix him up. I could tell his health was failing even more, but you helped him find the peace to cope with it. You treated him the night before he died. The way Lee Roy looked at me after you left, the way he was holding your hand that day, I feel Lee Roy knew it was the last time he would see you. There was such a calm and serene feeling in his room, until it made me cry. The night he died I can say I saw him die in PEACE! The look on his face told me what he could not say in words. It told me that he had accepted what was happening, he knew he was dying, and he was at peace with it. And at that moment I *was filled with tears of joy because I knew that the EDINA energy work had made this "peace" possible for this man who had for so very long suffered from his wartime experiences.*

The events that happened after Lee Roy's death were miraculous! Countless hummingbirds hovered outside his window for about a month! The Butterflies were there too, plentiful in their splendor! There is a deep sense of calmness I still feel when I go in his room to this very day!

Lee Roy initially was a skeptic, but he turned into a believer; he actually believed this energy work to be real, and it is.

Susie Brown

The above testimonials are just a few of the kinds of experiences E.D.I.N.A. initiates and their clients have had. The primary goal of E.D.I.N.A. is to assist humanity in this process called ascension. But first we must be healed in body, mind and spirit. The Ankenash say that E.D.I.N.A. is shamanism for the twenty-first century and beyond, and that this system will evolve, more will come into being, as we need it.

The Ankenash will work alongside the client/practitioner, or with us as individuals when we connect to The Ankenash all by ourselves—gradually healing us on all levels while reconnecting our 12 strand RNA/DNA whenever they are summoned. They are also helping us out by minimizing the uncomfortable side-effects of the ascension process.

Chapter 2
The First Appearance of The Ankenash

I must have been in a light trance state when I first saw the five of them standing in my treatment room. Normally I do go into a trance fairly quickly while working on anyone. As I recall, I was doing a Reiki massage treatment at the time—I do not know who it was I was working on; I wish I could recall. I have heard it said that often the most important days of our lives seem ordinary at the time, and we do not even realize until later that this particular day was significant. The day that these extra-dimensional beings first appeared was just that sort of day. I casually noticed one day that five beings looking very different than the usual spirits who always joined me in the healing room showed up—seemingly from out of nowhere. At first I just watched them "out of the corner of my eye," metaphorically speaking. I had never heard of tall, extra-dimensional beings before, although I now know that they also have appeared to others in the healing setting. But I certainly did not have the slightest inkling of a clue about anything like that at the time.

It's also impossible to pinpoint exactly even the exact year that it was I first saw them. I do clearly remember my first impression of them, what I thought they looked like. I was accustomed to Light Beings who were golden in color and of the same size and shape as humans. These new ones were tall blue-grey Light Beings—and I do mean tall. Appearing as beams of light, not shaped like people at all, they extended far out above the roof of the house I was working in at the time. This was, I think, in approximately 1998.

To give a bit of background, in March of the prior year I had opened a small metaphysical shop and bookstore in Houston, Texas, called "Hot Pink Lotus, Gifts of Higher Consciousness for Body, Mind and Spirit." In a small room in the back of the quaint old house, I had set up my treatment room and massage table. In those days, I was doing an Esalen style of Swedish massage coupled with Reiki. When these tall blue "people" showed up, I had been doing massages for nine years and Reiki for about twelve years. More importantly, though, I had been meditating in one form or another since 1975.

Regular daily meditation changes everything in a person, especially the brainwave pattern. This then affects the energy that comes out of the hands. A calmer energy is emitted from the small chakras in the palm of the hands in a regular meditator than the energy coming from a non-meditator's hands. Because of that, a person will also become more profoundly peaceful or relaxed when they are touched by someone who is a long-time meditator.

The brain wave frequency is affected by the state of mind; the state of mind and the consciousness are affected by meditation. The touch principle involved is similar to that of the galvanic skin response. This skin response is what is measured in an attempt to determine truth or falsehood via the lie detector test. So, the vibrational frequency coming from the hands of the healer or therapist is a very real and measurable thing.

Every time I touched people in the healing setting, no matter what the stated technique I was using, Reiki energy began flowing through my hands to the client as well. I could feel it flowing. It required no decision or intention, it just happened. I believed, and still do, that there were people whose Guides or Higher Selves sent them to me because they wanted them to also get energy healing and benefit from my many years of meditation. Otherwise, they would not have chosen to come see me. Saying it another way, they were intuitively guided to me, whether they knew it or not. Most were unaware of what Reiki was in the early 1990s when I started doing massages, although I knew that they could feel it. They said things like that I had the softest hands they had ever felt, or that my touch was unbelievably smooth. I feel certain that they were trying to express that they could perceive something was different about the touch. None of the other massage therapists I knew were Reiki initiates much less Reiki Masters, so I assumed that was why the touch felt different. My clients tried to express this difference in words, but they had difficulty. I said little beyond thanking them for the compliments.

I tried not to get into conversations about things like energy and vibrations and metaphysical or weird things; I was pretty sure most of them would not come back out of fear or confusion about what I was doing. Anything out of the ordinary was usually seen as witchy or dangerous in those days. People feared what they did not understand. One poor stressed-out woman who was a member of a fringe fundamentalist religious organization asked me after about the third massage if I were doing something she did not know about, because her religion forbade anything other than exactly what her religion allowed. I told her she had better not come back then, because there was something very spiritual going on, and that I could not stop it from happening. I said I hoped she would think for herself and keep coming, but that I suspected that what happened in my healing room was exactly the kind of thing her religion feared most. It was spiritual, but not religious. She never returned. I felt sad for her, because she wanted to return. She felt better when she was coming to see me, but her religion would not allow it. And she could not buck that system. This was her unique path, though, and it was not for me to interfere. Everyone is on his/her own path to perfection—it is not mine to judge or control.

By the time the tall blue beings came to me I was primarily seeing massage and/or Reiki clients. Some came just for Reiki. I had shamanic training from the Foundation for Shamanic Studies as well, so there were also Soul Retrievals or Power Animal Retrieval sessions. I was also doing some past life readings as taught to me by the Archangel Gabriel in the mid- 1980s. But most of my clients were simply Swedish massage clients, or there for cranio-sacral therapy or myofascial release. This was in the early 1990s.

I admit freely there was a lot of confusion for me the first years I did massage. I was living in Austin right after my divorce in those days. I could not understand why I was being asked to do something as simple as massage therapy, which I felt almost anyone could do. I believe now that when we are gifted at something, it seems so easy anyone could do it. Often we do not understand things except in retrospect. I now understand that doing massages was good for me. The experience healed me in many ways. In addition to relaxing complete strangers and thereby helping them reduce their disease-causing stress levels, I was helping with their spiritual growth—due to their picking up on the vibratory frequency resulting from the many years of meditation. Working silently in my personal monastery of massage also helped me with my own spiritual growth. Why? Because I was in a trance state working with my eyes closed for many hours per day. Essentially, I was meditating for hours upon hours daily; this benefited me as well as my clients.

Because of this eyes-closed in-trance practice following my fifteen years of meditation at that point, I effortlessly saw Light Beings in the healing room—almost from the start of my practice in May of 1990. I never expected this to happen. I was not looking for it because I had never even heard a whisper of such a thing happening to anyone. Yet there they were. Some seemed to be milling about. Some were working on the client's auric field, both near and far. Occasionally one of them would stand behind me, and reach his arms and hands through my arms and hands, and then reach on down inside the client's body. I was not sure precisely what they were doing inside the body, but it felt completely safe. I knew with a knowing that was utterly inexplicable that I could trust them unreservedly. I suppose since I knew that Reiki Masters in Spirit came around when we did Reiki, the Light Beings I was seeing didn't seem that strange. At the same time, I also simultaneously dismissed these visions as my imagination.

When I first began doing massage with Reiki, it was unthinkable to me to talk about things like this. I would have been viewed as a madwoman almost everywhere in those days. Again, I was not even that certain the beings were not all in my head, either. I observed it all without judgment, but never spoke of it to anyone—not one single person, at least none that I can recall. Looking back, I was totally in the now whenever I was doing a massage/Reiki session. I did not speak of it when a realtor in his fifties came to me and told me he'd previously had heart problems, but after one of my massage sessions he was healed. According to his cardiologist, there was simply no sign left of the heart disease. The client had himself re-tested shortly after our session, because he felt something change inside his heart while he was on the table. Tests showed that the problem with his heart had healed over. I was not sure I completely accepted this, and if it were true, I doubted it had anything to do with me. He came to tell me though, and brought me a bottle of Kahlua from a recent trip Mexico, because I had mentioned that I liked it. But I never saw him again. I think he was grateful yet frightened at the same time. Often I have felt like an alien from outer space for being so different.

I did not yet know that healing could happen spontaneously. I did not know that certain people had the capacity to spontaneously emit or transmit healing energies from their bodies to others in the form of scalar waves, at least, that is what is now believed by scientists who study this kind of thing. This had been happening to me for many years before I found out why I sometimes heated up like a furnace while working on clients. I would break into a sweat without much exertion. I experienced it for a long while before I heard a plausible explanation for what was going on. But please know that even if a person does not normally emit the spontaneous healing force, he or she can do energy medicine! Everyone I have ever trained has had the ability to contact The Ankenash and do this work. I mention the body's heating up in case anyone else is doing spontaneous healing and does not know what that heat is.

Getting back to the Light Beings in my treatment room, the first Light Beings I had been exposed to were shaped like humans and were of about the same size. But they were translucent, and made either of white or golden yellow light. I did not see any wings. It did not occur to me to look for them, either. As mentioned earlier, I would get reports of miraculous healings from some of the clients we worked upon together. It was my nature to receive this information with a bit of curiosity as well as skepticism. I did not believe that I was actually "doing" anything special or magical. I suspected there might be some kind of strange magic going on, but I felt sure that it happened in spite of me, and not because of me. In retrospect I must say that at the time, I was completely unaware of the enormity of what was actually going on in the healing room. I was living mostly from the conscious mind, innocently believing at the time that this was the only thing I could trust.

My conscious mind did not readily accept the notion of strange and mystical things occurring at the tips of anyone's fingers, or in the air around them, even when the evidence clearly pointed to that. I chalk it up to early conditioning. Logically, I knew that many people believed that Reiki worked, and I was aware from experience that it could be felt even if one did not know what it was—I had tried experiments early on, upon clueless friends, asking if I could put my hand on an injured knee for example—and then had them ask what that strange sensation coming from my hand was. Yet oddly I did not think for a moment that anything special was going on in my massage room. And that is okay. Humility is a good thing.

And so even though I regularly saw translucent golden-yellow Light Beings in the healing room, on one level, I also simultaneously dismissed it as my imagination. Like most people raised in the 1950s and 60s, when as a child I had tried to tell adults about this kind of thing which I saw, I had been told it was not real. It was "merely imagination." Of course, I now know there is nothing "mere" about the imagination of a human being.

It was a magnificent confirmation for me when several years after I had started massage work that I saw Barbara Brennan's book, "Hands of Light." This book had color illustrations of almost exactly what I had been seeing for years in my healing room. Had I not learned from seeing those images in Barbara's book that other people were also having precisely the same visions, I might never have been open or receptive to the immensely tall blue beings when they showed up. I might have dismissed them as not real, or not allowed myself to become fully aware of them. Certainly I would not have listened to them when they answered questions inside my head, carrying on a conversation telepathically. It is truly uncanny how the sequence of things seems to have been orchestrated so carefully—when viewed in retrospect.

Chapter 3

Something Strange in the Room

I was fortunate to have had a massage instructor in Austin who at one point mentioned that someday we would experience the "Zen of Massage." After that began to happen to me, I was sure she was talking about these trance states which made something as supremely boring as massage bearable day after day. As an educated intellectual, I did not know in the beginning how anyone could do this kind of work for very long, but my guidance told me to go to massage school, so I did. Then after I began going into trance states daily, I got into the groove and enjoyed it immensely.

This daily trance state made it easier to relax and allow for the possibility of Light Beings in the room. After a few weeks of the blue ones showing up, I wondered silently to myself who or what this new appearance was. I heard immediately an answer, "We are the blah-blah-blah."

"What did they say?" I wondered in my head. They repeated their answer telepathically. I had to listen closely and ask them to repeat it quite a few times until I understood their name. It was a very odd-sounding and unfamiliar word. I realize now that it was also a completely new language to me so I had no point of reference. Each time they said their name, I was sure I would remember it, but did not. Like with a dream, we think after a trance we will remember what happened or what was said, but we do not. After asking them to repeat their name casually over several days, it finally occurred to me to place a piece of paper and a pencil on the table where I stored my massage tools before I began to work on my first client that day. The work table was within reach of my massage table. I decided that the next time they appeared I would stop and write their name down. So I did. In mid-massage and with one hand still on my client's back, I reached over with the other hand and wrote down the name: "The Ankenash." They then told me their name was derived from three letters of the Kabballah, and that if I looked at a book about those letters, I would know from exactly which letters their name was derived. The name is not exactly those three letters strung together verbatim, it is derived from the three letters.

Extremely curious as to what I would find, I went to a book-store that day and found a few books on the Kabballah, a subject which I had never been even mildly curious about before. I had never to the best of my memory even cracked open a book on this subject, even though I am an avid read-er. As I flipped through the names and meanings of the let-ters, I easily found the three that I was sure were the right ones. Ayin, Kalph and Aleph. The book I consulted at the time had the meanings as Eye, Palm of Hand, and Flame, Diagnosis or Final Resolution. At least, that was what caught my eye first. I now know that those three letters have a vast multiplicity of meanings.

Ayin can also mean the illuminating principle behind the act of conception. It is the closest letter to the Source. It means that life, whether it is physical or spiritual, comes from the same process. Kalph can also mean, besides palm of hand, the final attainment of individual existence as conceived in the beginning (ascension? return to source?). It can mean the archetypal container, as the human form is the arche-typal container of the human spirit. Aleph can mean primal energy, ultimate oneness and ultimate nothingness. It is that which brings into form that which is formless; the letter that has no sound; referring to the emptiness out of which life vividly flashes into being. Needless to say, this began to sound like very heady stuff. But I vacillated between "This is heady," and "I am full of malarkey—I must be making this up somehow." But *how* was I making this up?

This experience with the Kaballah is a perfect example of how, from the very beginning, and in spite of my doubts, I was guided by The Ankenash. First it was to a book that told me the meaning of the letters from which their name was derived. It explained enough that I could extrapolate that the letters meant a flame that came from an eye which exists in the center of the palm of the hand and which creates a diagnosis and final resolution (healing?). I was stunned. I could not be making this up. I repeat, I had never before opened a book on the Kaballah; I never even had the vaguest interest in that subject. Yet wasn't a flame in the palm of the hand which heals/diagnoses/resolves rather what Reiki was? Seriously? Light (flame) that comes out of the palm of the hand? I had seen numerous Tibetan Thanka paintings with eyeballs painted in the palms of hands, and upon the palms of feet. I knew exactly what that meant. I had practiced shamanism for over ten years by then. I knew that one could look inside a person's body by placing the palm of a hand on the body and with closed eyes, look inside the body using the palm of either or both hands like an eye. I also knew, because a Tibetan Rinpoche Lama once had come to see me in Houston for massages, that there was a sect of Tibetan Buddhism which practiced shamanism. He and I had talked about Tibetan Buddhist shamanism for hours because he noticed shamanic tools in my treatment room. Beyond that, I also had seen flames coming from the palm of my hand at one time—many years earlier.

Once in about 1982, I accidentally burned my eyelid trying to wax my own eyebrows, I placed my right palm over my eye for over an hour while simultaneously tending to my two young sons as they got ready for bed. The other eye remained open so I could keep an eye on my three and six-year-old sons. I got a few minutes' pause while they were in the big, white claw-footed tub of our huge bathroom in our Victorian house in Galveston.

As I sat in my low white wicker chair near the tub, I was near enough to the boys to feel safe covering both eyes while my sweet little boys splashed and played with toys. My attention drifted for a moment to my hand and burned eyelid. Shocked, I realized that I was seeing golden yellow undulating flames, viewed as if I were looking down from above the flame. It was definitely coming from my palm. At the time I had no idea that this would be confirmation of something vastly more important almost twenty years later. It seemed pretty significant all by itself at the time. Reiki came out of the hand like a flame! I had seen it with my own open eyes! Seeing things with my eyes closed did not amaze me like seeing them open-eyed did for some reason.

Thinking again about the meanings for the three letters of the Kabballah, I knew that I could never have made that up on my own. I realized with a shock that this was not just my imagination! Something was going on here that was beyond me, beyond my small self. I was being telepathically communicated with by intelligent if semi-visible beings capable of sending me to find a book to explain further what I needed to know about them.

Hedging my bets, however, I did not tell anyone at all about this phenomenon called The Ankenash at that time. I just continued to allow it all to unfold in my healing room, observing the phenomenon without judgment. The Ankenash began to suggest to me that I use Tibetan bowls and specific stones in my healing work. They would tell me what to place where on each client, and it was different for each of them. The Ankenash would let me know what bowls to play, what rhythm, and in what sequence.

Clients began to show up who just wanted me to work on them with Reiki and the stones and bowl sounds. I began to add stones to my healing room collection, going into my shop area and picking them up as guided, thinking they would go back into the shop later to be sold, but they never have. I now have about ten stones for each chakra to use as guided. Sometimes the stones go to places other than chakras, too. I would begin these sessions by smudging the room I was working in, myself, and the client.

Theresa was one client who showed up in my shop again and again in those early years to enjoy the energy in the shop, to get readings from me, to buy the jewelry I made and my Arkansas crystals and such. She was a fit, beautiful, well-dressed blonde, and smart—yet with a hard edge. I suspected she had some very difficult experiences in her life which had toughened her up a bit. My heart was touched by the vulnerability that she tried so hard to protect with her "tough girl" act. I could see right through her act, having had a similar act of my own once. One day I urged her to let me work on her so she could experience energy medicine. I told her it would be a free session. She hesitated, but reluctantly agreed.

Theresa got onto my table, and I placed stones on her chakras, put Tibetan bowls on her body or on the table as instructed. Then I began working in her aura and on her body as directed by The Ankenash—toning with the bowls, my tingshas and bell and dorje as they instructed. The Ankenash had come in to work on her in the expanded realms at the same time. As I placed stones around her body and on chakras her muscles began to twitch uncontrollably after a few minutes.

After a few minutes she asked me, "Who are the Beings who recently came into the room? They are so huge!"

I was shocked; she had never given any clue before that she had this level of intuitive ability. I queried, "You can see them?" She replied that yes, she could sense intuitively that they were there. I told her they were called The Ankenash. And I continued to work on her. Almost immediately her body had begun to twitch all over. She was having small uncontrollable muscle spasms. At some point this smart, tough cookie of a career woman began to sob uncontrollably on my table, but reported later that there were no thoughts in her head at all. Theresa reports that I did not react at all, but just kept on working. She says that it made it easier for her to just focus on her own release work and cry without distraction until she was finished. She was very grateful that all I did was to casually slide a box of tissues I placed upon a tall stool close enough to her that she could grab a couple of them as needed. She was not sure what she cried about, but that is not necessary in release work. Sometimes grief or sorrow or other emotions trapped for years in our muscles or other tissues just needs to be released! If it is not released, it can cause disease later on. When I was finished working and Theresa got off the table, she was hooked on energy medicine. And she also insisted that she pay for the session. Years later she would tell me that this experience was a turning point for her, and that she realized on the table that day that there were just some things in this Universe you could not explain.

A few years later she wanted to send a gentleman friend in for a session, and she asked me to do that thing with the stones and bowls, not BodyTalk or Psych-K, so he could feel something immediately. I was very surprised, and thought she must have an ability to feel energy that was beyond my own. On the other hand, I also began to wonder if those stones which had been in my healing room all those years had picked up special energies from being there. So one afternoon I laid down on the table and put my own stones on my chakras, and had a very big surprise! I could feel energy moving down my legs from my second chakra area and out the bottoms of my feet and down into the ground below. The stones had indeed picked up energy from being stored in my healing room. And they were working on me. Many years after that I read a book which confirmed that objects in a meditation environment pick up on that energy and transmit it, even if they have been moved over a thousand miles away from the meditation room and their frequencies re-measured. (from Lynne McTaggart – "The Intention Experiment")

Theresa has since developed her own intuitive abilities further and has begun walking her spiritual path as guided by her own Spiritual Guides and Higher Self, and it has been a rare and fascinating journey. Still a career woman, she has studied E.D.I.N.A., and does E.D.I.N.A. daily on herself, on her pets and a select few close friends.

Doing this kind of work alongside The Ankenash with a select group of individuals went on for a couple of years before the next stage began, when I began learning the Body-Talk System, and The Ankenash announced to me one day that they would "step aside for a while," so I could learn this new system.

Chapter 4
A Glimpse of Home

In addition to being of a different color and shape from previous Light Beings I had seen in the healing room, these blue Starbeings were additionally different in that they consistently arranged themselves in a pattern around the healing table that was very precise. Wherever I stood, they moved to create a pattern around the table that left two of us on one side of the table, two on the other side of the table and one each at the head and foot of the table. I say "us" because it not only gave the appearance of group work, but when I wondered about it, they told me that it truly was group work. They referred to the pattern as "the six of us." The pattern reminded me of an abbreviated version of the Tree of Life from sacred geometry or the Kaballah. When I thought their calling this pattern "the six of us" was odd, they answered that I was actually one of them.

When I wondered why I never knew about this before, they answered that it had not yet been time for me to remember. I realized that it might indeed have been overwhelming. Often if we know too much too soon, we can simply shut down, or run "hide under the bed." And we cannot get very much done while hiding under the bed.

The Ankenash explained that there was a more expanded aspect of myself asleep in a special room in a kind of temple at their home base. She was sleeping because about eighty percent of her energy was going to me as her incarnation with a special job to do. They further explained that their home base was located at Sirius-B. When they told me this, with a gasp, I suddenly flashed back to an incident which had happened when I was in my mid-thirties, about fifteen years earlier.

My family and I arrived home after dark one evening during the sweltering damp heat of an August Texas Gulf coast summer. The air was thick with mosquitoes. We pulled into our driveway in the Silk Stocking Historic District in Galveston, stopping the car in the driveway next to the house. As we got out of the car I happened to glance straight up. I froze in my tracks, gasping. My attention was riveted upon a star in the sky that was so enormous I wondered if it were a satellite or even a starship. No stars were ever so large, at least not in my experience. Almost instantly out of my mouth came the trembling words, "Is that Sirius?" I do not know where those words came from as at the time I had no idea there was a star named Sirius. While pronouncing those words, something deep stirred within me, and I had an immense longing, a homesickness that was by far the deepest well of homesickness I had ever known possible. I knew in an instant that I was from Sirius, and that I wanted desperately to go home. But I could not go yet, and I knew that just as immediately. I was crestfallen and simultaneously grateful to have seen a glimpse of home again, even though I did not know why I felt this way.

In answer to my question, my husband mumbled something like, "I don't know what that is. Who cares?" Stars were just not his thing. And I was left alone with my deep feeling of longing. Many things could not be shared with him or anyone else. I puzzled over this for a while, and with nothing further to attach to it, I let it go. Although I did not know this at the time, the incident was quite securely tucked away in vivid detail somewhere in memory, ready to emerge again when the time was right.

That time was right that day in my healing room, when The Ankenash told me, many years later, that part of me was asleep on Sirius giving about eighty percent of her energy to me as an incarnation, because I had important work to do. I had absolutely no idea what the serious work was that I was to do. I was also mildly curious about this higher aspect of myself in another star system, but there was no further information forthcoming at that time.

As it turns out, Sirius-B, which is The Ankenash' home base star, is not visible to us on Earth at all without telescopes. What we refer to as Sirius is a triune star, with Sirius-A being the large, bright visible one. Sirius-B and Sirius-C rotate around the big bright one. However, I do not think anyone but the Dogon Tribe in Africa were actually aware of the second two stars at the time of the incident in my driveway in the 1980s. All that was known at that time was that Sirius was really big, and that it had a most unusual orbit.

Countless times I have received confirmation of things in strange ways, with time as no consideration at all. This was not the only time. Many more continue to occur even now.

Chapter 5
The Artist and Mother

Many things led to my being in that massage room in Houston when The Ankenash showed up. I had to feel the deep despair of not living my Soul's purpose. I had to pursue the cultural dream of success and achieve it before I saw its hollowness for me. Otherwise, I might have been longing for such a life indefinitely, having experienced a wild boomerang of affluence followed by periods of poverty growing up. The experience of poverty leaves its mark on a child—in my case it made me ambitious to succeed by the cultural standards just to feel safe. I did not want to worry about how to pay the rent, put food on the table or how to get health care or medicine when I or my loved ones were ill—not ever again. I worked hard to put that behind me. And I did that.

At one point in my life in Galveston, I was a board member of both the national volunteer organization, the Junior League, and of the local art non-profit, "Galveston Arts!" as well as the wife of a successful trial lawyer whom I had put through school. I was the managing General Partner in a limited partnership owning historical commercial properties. I was restoring, leasing and managing our Victorian-era commercial properties, the largest of which was in the Strand National Landmark Historic District in downtown Galveston. I was responsible for everything in that business, although my husband had set up the business model and structure. My input was not allowed in structuring the business. That sense of not being able to control what I was held responsible for was just one of the crushing situations in which I found myself toward the end of my marriage. It felt at the time as though I had jumped out of an ocean-liner in the middle of the sea with no flotation device, not knowing how to swim. The crashing economy in the late 1980s parallel the shuttle crash which made everyone up the road at NASA nervous about coming to Galveston to spend tourist dollars on the Strand did not help this situation any.

I had been married for over eighteen years to a man I put through five years of college, including three years of law school, having also put myself through grad school simultaneously. I had also worked my way through undergraduate school as well. I say I put him through school because I was the only one of us who worked while we both were attending school. During the Galveston years I was also a practicing artist with a Master of Fine Arts degree. I exhibited nationally and internationally in juried shows, and locally in gallery shows. Frequently I was a prize winner in the national juried shows. I did a lot of volunteer work as that was expected of the wife of a small-town superstar trial lawyer in those days. All that plus raising children kept me extremely busy, but did not keep me from becoming miserably unhappy. Something mysterious was terribly wrong, and I knew it for years before I finally figured out what it was. Raising my children and making art were the only things that satisfied or sustained me. The only elements of my life which fulfilled me were loving and nurturing my two precious sons and making art.

I was completely unable to grasp at that time the concept that the art was a spiritual expression. During a time when I was an agnostic in reaction to an upbringing in a rabidly fundamentalist, fear-mongering church, art was indeed my only spiritual expression. I was actually channeling art in the late 1960s through the 1980s, but did not yet have in my vocabulary the word "channeling." I referred to what I was doing as "connecting to the collective unconscious." My major professor in grad school at the University of North Tex-as, Claudia Webb Betti, was an aficionado of psychologist Carl Jung, and she taught me that phrase. I thank heaven for that. I simply had no other words for what was happen-ing. Many times I would sit down in front of a blank canvas or sheet of paper with no idea at all of what was to come. I would just allow it to flow out of me with no real under-standing of where the images came from. It was like being inside a waking dream.

Often I would look back years later at my paintings or draw-ings and see that these artworks were prophetic in nature. They symbolically foretold events I had no way of knowing about before they occurred. Sometimes the images were quite strange, like series of works with people who had beaks and wings, but who also looked in all other ways like humans. In one colored pencil drawing one of these winged beings appeared, floating mid-air in front of the house across the street from ours. Smoke rose in a large, men-acing-looking black cloud from the chimney of the house, and the winged being held one hand up with the forefin-ger pointing upward, as if in warning. I called it "Bird Lady's Warning." A few months later there was a major hurricane, Alicia, the first direct hit in Galveston in over twenty years. The ominous black cloud was pointing at the direction from where the storm came, too.

Where did these images come from? No one I knew talk-ed about spiritual or metaphysical things back then. The only word I had that acknowledged my differentness, and which I owned for myself, was the word artist. I had not re-ally claimed the word mystic or even psychic for myself. And psychic actually still is not a word that appeals to me; I pre-fer the word "intuitive".

I liked the words mystic and medium. In fact I had taken a

black and white photo of myself in my mid-twenties, using a timer on the camera, sitting in a pose with my opened hands next to my face palms facing forward, and under it I placed the quote from artist Marcel Duchamp, "The Artist is like a mediumistic being who, from the labyrinth beyond time and space, seeks his way out to a clearing." This statement deeply resonated with me, but I did not know why. Much later I realized the posture is one that the Hathors use in many of the depictions of them on temple walls in Egypt. I now use that pose when the Hathors come into in my healing sessions these days, and I teach it to my students. I had no way to know what that posture meant back then. I only knew that it appealed to me. It felt really good to be in that posture. I realize now that not only did I work with the Hathors in several past lives in Ancient Egypt but that I have had past lives as a Hathor as well.

My husband thought that it was an odd photo, the one with my hands beside my face, palms forward, yet he liked it. He was not unfamiliar with my strangeness. He knew I was psychic/intuitive when he married me. In fact, when we were dating he had told me that I carried the "Cassandra Curse" and told me what his understanding of that meant. He said that I would accurately predict the future, others would not believe me, and later when what I said came true, they would not be able to remember that I had predicted this in the first place. I thought that was a cruel thing to say. Yet it was not. In fact, it was just the unvarnished truth. That is how it has usually been with those close to me, the ones who matter most. There was more to the Cassandra Curse that I would not learn for another forty years, but I digress. My children's father was a powerful teacher for me in many ways.

One of the lessons was in teaching me how important it

was to trust my perceptions. We must do this for ourselves despite what others we love say to us about the subject. Our sensory perceptions—sight, smell, hearing, taste and touch—are our connections to reality, whether they be ordinary senses for the regular folks, or the added boost of extraordinary senses for the psychics, mediums and mystics among us. If we cannot trust our senses to report accurately about our reality, what can we trust? How difficult will it be for us to remain sane? Fortunately I managed to remain in touch with reality, but instead became deeply depressed. Yet I did not know why. Now I know it was because there were important people in my life telling me that my perceptions were not true. And that can drive a person insane if it goes on long enough. This concept is beautifully and accurately illustrated in the old film, "Gaslight."

And of course, depression is a very common form of mental illness. At least that is what the psychological community calls it. The spiritual community says it is the Soul trying to tell us something is wrong in our lives. I did succumb to depression for a while. Yet while depression can be biochemical in nature, when it is a signal from the Soul that something is wrong in our lives, it not only requires we make changes, it sometimes requires medication to reverse. Once it gets started, it can become biochemical. Depressed states can be brought on by external stimuli or depression can come from within. Psychologists call this exogenous and endogenous etiology respectively.

Additionally, when in graduate school in psychology in the later years of my marriage, I watched rats go mad as their rewards were gradually made less and less frequent. This is called "leaning the rewards"—making the rewards, or positive reinforcement, harder and harder to come by. No matter how hard they tried, they got fewer and fewer rewards for their efforts. Indeed, a major light went on in my head that summer. I was thankfully beginning to absorb a very important lesson. It was a painful one.

Over the years because of my intuitive abilities, many strange and exotic--sometimes exciting and wonderful—things have happened to me. Yet when I reported them to others, in adulthood as well as in childhood, I was rebuked and told this was not reality. I was told that I simply had a very vivid imagination; I was constantly told that I was "living in a dream world" as a child. So for the most part as a result of these experiences, I have always felt very different from other people, as if I could never fit in or trust anyone with my reality. And that is a very lonely place to live. Some of those events were just odd things, which I have never quite understood, some were exciting and fun, and some are occurrences that made sense only later. Then there are those bizarre events which have occurred and were immediately crystal clear in their meaning.

It was precisely this propensity to mystical experiences that was the most powerful indicator of my strangeness, and why I would never ultimately feel comfortable in the Galveston lifestyle. It felt stifling to me. People lived there the way the rest of Texas lived fifty years prior. In Galveston, people still wore tuxedos to dinner parties at posh old homes when I first arrived in 1976, and never, ever talked openly about the ghosts who co-inhabited with them in their homes. There quite a number of the ghost-spirits, too, especially in the East End where we later lived—where all the historic Victorian homes are located. I suspect that more so than in any city of comparable size in America there are ghosts there. I believe that this was mainly because of the "class five" hurricane that landed one night in September of 1900 with absolutely no warning, killing between five and ten thousand people in one night. Ghosts truly overran that place. Each time I left town and returned I could feel an overwhelming heaviness. I had no words for it; I thought the feeling that overcame me was just a result of the ugly billboards that lined the street leading into town from the mainland. I had nothing else to pin it on! Almost everyone I knew seemingly ignored these lost souls who were living among us until I began teaching meditation in my living room, and then people began to speak in whispers about it in the group or else privately to me. Certainly I felt that I had them in my house.

Fortunately, a gentleman friend of ours confirmed my own "house ghosts" to me privately without my even asking. Right after we moved in, he caught me alone in the kitchen briefly once when he and his family had come to visit us. He reported that he saw both of the women I had been seeing, confirming for me that indeed there were two women. He saw them wearing the same clothing as I saw, and being mother and daughter. He said something was wrong with the daughter, and that she never had children so she loved to watch mine play. He thought maybe she died of leukemia, since her image seemed especially pale. I was to later learn from a much older neighbor that an older lady and her retarded adult daughter had lived in my house for a very long time, perhaps forty years, with the old lady's son. He was an auditor who worked for the City of Galveston. My male friend who saw these women in spirit form was also a deacon in his church and later politically active, so he did not talk about this kind of thing often. I remained quite lonely in my differentness.

By the time I finally got out of Galveston I was a nervous wreck for many reasons. I truly needed that time alone in the woods of Westlake Hills, going into meditative trances every day in my treatment room. I needed the six years of "down time" to heal from the trauma of staying in that difficult situation that took me so many years finally to release. It was a slow, painful thing, and it had almost killed me before I finally reached down deep enough to find the courage to leave. I fully take the blame for that. For many reasons I had a hard time letting go. It was a harsh lesson; it was a lesson in trusting my perceptions, and it was a lesson in valuing myself in spite of all the devaluation going on around me. This most of all was a lesson in believing that I could steer my own ship. It was among the first time of many to come yet in my life that I felt the fear and did something anyway. I am very grateful for the lesson: "Feel the fear and do it anyway!" It has served me well in later years! Looking back, I can see that my childrens' father was one of my greatest teachers. And I thank him.

Chapter 6

Synchronicity

After those six years in the monastery of my massage treatment room in Austin I returned to Houston, which is just north of Galveston. A few years after that I found myself in the treatment room in the Heights of Houston where The Ankenash first showed up. They worked with me for about two years until, as I mentioned earlier, I became acquainted with the BodyTalk System. At that time they told me they were going to step aside so that I could learn the BodyTalk System. I was not sure what that meant. But I was so excited about BodyTalk that I moved forward with my studies, taking my first class in March of 2002. Why was I so excited?

I had had a remarkable personal healing experience in 2001 with BodyTalk at a time when I desperately needed healing from a spontaneous memory of a very traumatic past life. I had been spiraling emotionally downward until Donna Guthery did two sessions for me and completely healed my trauma. She had only studied BodyTalk's first two modules at that time, too. My only doubts about the BodyTalk System came from two bits of information.

First, I had heard from my former sister-in-law who had taken some of the classes that the founder and his wife expected everyone to embrace their spiritual beliefs sooner or later. Secondly, this BodyTalk experience was going to be about joining an organization. I had never really enjoyed being part of a group—I was not especially trusting of group dynamics at that time. And as far as my being told what to believe about spirituality, anyone who thinks they can tell me what to believe is in for a really big, unpleasant surprise. I am not interested in religions or in dogma or in following anyone else's rules, unless the reasons for the rules make logical sense to me. I am interested only in making a direct, mind-to-mind connection to the Source of Creation. Nothing else interests me. I assumed the pressure of the Veltheims' beliefs would sooner or later be a problem. But I wanted to learn as much as I could about this style of healing before it did.

So I began taking classes and practiced BodyTalk for about five and a half years before The Ankenash came back. During that time via the BodyTalk Forum online I was able to compare my healing abilities to that of other people across the globe. I was astounded to learn that I was a highly gifted healer. Many times I did sessions that resulted in healing the supposedly incurable. My results were among the best in the world. I got the information in my sessions intuitively. Additional BodyTalk methods would show up in my sessions which I shared on the Forum at the founder's request, and which were picked up by other BodyTalkers. These became a part of the BodyTalk system. John Veltheim privately thanked me for my contribution to the matrix of BodyTalk. At one point I posted early in my participation on the Forum that John was not creating BodyTalk, but that it already existed and was revealing itself to him/us. He also thanked me profoundly for that in private: I came to love him like a brother. As a result of my involvement with this system, I began to see myself more clearly, and to begin to suspect that I had something important to contribute to the field of energy medicine. And due to my involvement with the Forum online, when I went to the BodyTalk International Conference one year, I was treated like a rock star by the other participants who had been following my posts. This boosted my self-esteem. I got a fresh and much-needed, clearer perspective on myself. Without this experience in the Body-Talk Commuity I would not ever have had the confidence to bring E.D.I.N.A. energy medicine to the planet. For this experience with the BodyTalk community worldwide, I am truly appreciative.

Then the next phase of my life began. In late 2006 I had an astrological reading from the famous astrologist Robert Wilkinson, whom I had initially met in Austin in 1990. I rediscovered him surfing the web when I stumbled across his brilliant "Aquarius Papers" blog. I remembered strangely prophetic things he had said back when I first met him and got a reading. One of them was that I was born a shaman. This was before I had trained in shamanism, or even knew that anyone still practiced this "antiquated" system. I absolutely did not appreciate the depth of what he was saying until a few years later, when I studied shamanism with Sandra Ingerman, Educational Director of the Foundation for Shamanic Studies. But because of that experience earlier with Robert, I listened closely to what he said when I found him again in 2006. One of the things he said was that something of major importance to my life was about to happen. This was something that would mean, as Robert put it, that it was "time to put on the show for the rest of your life." He said this would happen between mid-March and mid-April of 2007. And that, as it later turned out, is precisely when The Ankenash unexpectedly returned. Yet I did not make the connection to his prediction until about halfway through their instructions to me.

In the pre-dawn hours one morning in mid-March, 2007, as I sat sipping green tea in my easy chair as was my custom each morning, the five of them just showed up in my living room and began speaking to me. I was beyond surprised. I had not thought about them for quite a while except in passing. And here they were, just appearing all of a sudden one day with no warning, talking to me again. They began saying some very interesting things about healing and energy. I murmured things like, "Hmmm...that's interesting!" and wondering why they were telling me these fascinating things. At that point one of them said, "Write it down, Lois." And then I snapped to attention. They wanted me to write it down. Never before had they suggested I write anything down. And here they were appearing again, but this time not in my healing room! This was a completely different setting. "Of course," I thought, "this is not just an inter-dimensional chat session. I am to pay attention here, and take notes!"

Quickly it became clear that they were dictating a new form of energy medicine to me. I could hear their words very easily, but again to be clear, this was telepathic speech. So I got out some paper and a pen and began to write the things down that I was hearing. Early on I heard a new word in my head: EDINA. I thought that was strange, since I already knew their names: The Ankenash. So why was there a new word? I resisted it. I tried to ignore it, but it came back again and again until gave in and I wrote it down. As I looked at the word, it became clear what it meant. It was an acronm: Energy Dynamics for the Integration of Natural Attributes. The Ankenash explained that this form of energy medicine was to help us regain certain natural attributes which humans had not utilized for several thousands of years. It had somehow to do with the ascension process, they said. It additionally had to do with reconnecting our twelve strand RNA/DNA and with healing and somehow re-activating the Light Body.

This initial dictation went on for about a month—always early in the morning as I faced northwest—sitting in my leather recliner, my cup of green tea resting next to me on a side table, under the window onto my front porch. I could see birds and hanging plants from this chair once the sun began to peek over the horizon. It was a serene place to interact with these old friends.

Interestingly, each time The Ankenash would give me information, they would send rather immediate confirmation in the outer world. This occurred usually the same day; perhaps the next day. The confirmation might come in the form of a website a friend or client insisted I needed to see, one I stumbled upon looking for something else, or a book someone spontaneously brought to me. It could show up in the form of something said on the radio or television. It might come in the form of a class I took because I needed massage therapy continuing education units, and then when I got there the class information would be extremely similar to what The Ankenash had just been telling me about. The sources of their outer confirmation were varied and many. In fact, their sending Robert Wilkinson six months earlier to hint at their coming was a form of confirmation. His having told me that made it easier to trust that what was going on was real. I knew because of that reading that I should pay close attention to the event when it did happen.

The Ankenash had told me from the beginning in March of 2007 that I was destined to bring back to the world a form of healing humanity had known and practiced widely prior to The Fall. This technique had been fragmented into pieces with bits of the system spread out all over the globe. Many bits were preserved in shamanic techniques by the Indigenous Peoples of the earth. Other pieces were held by Chinese Medical Chi Gong tradition, and some of it was known by healers in India, South America and North American Indians and other peoples and locations as well. Certain techniques have been given to me directly by The Anke-nash; pieces they said were no longer held anywhere on Earth. Some techniques are completely new.

Of course, I wonder occasionally why I have been both thus burdened and thus honored. Several times I have asked them, "Why me?" They always answer with, "Why <u>not</u> you?" I simply have no comeback for that.

Chapter 7

Getting Permissions: The Sovereignty of the Soul

The Ankenash also reminded me of the basic tenets of spiritual healing. One of the primary tenets is that energy medicine or spiritual healing is always permission-based. While it is all right to pray for someone in a way that does not dictate the outcome—one which implies that the outcome be determined by Source (i.e. thy will be done)—healing is different. This belief is held by most traditions around the planet as well. The reason for this is that if I decide I know what is best for you and do a healing session for you without your permission, I am interfering with your Soul's Journey. This journey is a path which is completely unique to each of us, and one of the primary variables is our ability to choose and learn at the Soul level from those consequences. This ability to choose is also called "Free Will" and was given to us by the Creator. Thus it is absolutely sacrosanct. No human person knows what is better for you than does your own Soul. If I decide I know what is best for you, not only am I wrongly and presumptuously putting myself ahead of your Soul and Spirit Guides in importance, I am incurring some hefty negative karma for myself by violating your God given right to free will. You have the right to decide if you want my healing ministrations—everyone does. Maybe you prefer a different healer or method, or nothing at all. That is your right. This is true even if you are my adult child, spouse, sister, brother, mother, father, lover, neighbor, friend, co-worker or a total stranger.

Or perhaps your Soul determined that it wanted to experience multiple sclerosis, arthritis or heart disease as a way to learn a particular lesson(s) in this lifetime. If I decide that I know best and that you definitely need to be healed, and I work on you without your knowledge or permission, then I am interfering with the chosen path of your Soul. This goes way beyond presumptuous! Each and every Soul is absolutely sovereign. And if yours is a karmic illness which you decided prior to incarnating to experience for the purpose of learning and growth as a Soul, nothing any healer does will "heal" it unless your Soul is ready!

If you are wondering what to do if the sick person is a child or perhaps an unconscious adult, or even a pet, here is The Ankenash's answer. Ask the child's parent or legal guardian. Grandparents cannot give permission unless they are the legal guardians of that child. The same is true for the unconscious patient; ask for their medical guardian's permission, who is usually a spouse or parent. Naturally, you ask the pet's owner before working on a pet. As for plants or wild animals, use a "distance" technique to get their own permission.

I have heard others tell of healing modalities whose leaders encourage their students to practice with wild abandon on everyone and everything they encounter without any regard for permission: "See a homeless person on the street? Just clear them!" Personally, I would run like the wind to get away from any modality which allows such a disregard for the sovereignty of the Soul. However, that modality choice is up to the individual healing practitioner. I would never presume to tell anyone else which modality to use. We must each use our own inner guidance in making these decisions.

I would, however, sincerely suggest that you not practice E.D.I.N.A. without permission, because The Ankenash have charged me with the responsibility of seeing to it that everyone understands not to do that. They are gifting humanity with a powerful healing tool, one that heals quickly and efficiently far beyond anything else I have ever worked with, and it starts by the healing/balancing of the human Light Body. I know for sure they get to determine how this tool is used since it comes to us via them. I also deeply sense that it is a great honor and privilege to work alongside 12-dimensional Light Beings from Sirius-B in the healing room. And these highly evolved beings tell us unequivocally to get client permission. Period. They also tell me that if any individual healer does not respect the parameters of the method, The Ankenash will just not show up to work with that person any longer. Period. (There are ways to word asking for permission that do not include talking about invisible blue people.)

I had an associate early on who decided she did not need permission to heal others because a Being that she channeled stated that getting permission was not necessary. "Healing is like prayer," the spirit supposedly told my associate. I told her that particular spirit was not associated with E.D.I.N.A., so if she wanted to practice E.D.I.N.A., she needed permission. As a result, she decided to no longer practice E.D.I.N.A, deciding for some reason to follow the dictates of a spirit not associated with E.D.I.N.A. That is just how the river flows. She is on a different path than E.D.I.N.A. And it's okay. All roads lead to Source. It is not up to us to judge another person's path. Their journey is their own. We would all be wise to remember this and to respect that fact.

Regarding Reiki Permissions

For those who do not know, Reiki, probably the best known energy medicine at the time of this writing is a form of energy medicine which has been around for tens of thousands of years. After falling out of use several hundreds of years ago, it was rediscovered by a Japanese Christian educator, Mikao Usui, in the 1800s. Reiki requires that you get permission from the client before working on him or her, and not just "at a distance" permission. If the person is conscious, you are required to ask them for their permission to work on them. It is not appropriate (or fair) to go in "through the back door" and get permission at a distance or remotely. Getting remote permission when you can get conscious permission is called making an end-run around the permission rule.

As a Reiki Master since 1988, I have always told students laughingly, "No sneak-Reiki, please!" Sneak-Reiki would include things like drawing, from a distance, a Reiki symbol on a stranger's back in a public place. That argument she is having with her child or husband may be just what the two of them need at this time for their optimal spiritual growth! Healing without permission is clearly forbidden in Reiki.

When I started practicing Reiki way back in 1986 the very few of us who were doing Reiki all knew this fact. Over time, as Reiki has spread, many Reiki instructors have not continued to teach the original full body of the Reiki teachings, and there are some Reiki instructors and practitioners out there who were never told that getting permission is a sacred duty. But it definitely is.

I think it would be interesting to note at this point that The Ankenash tell me they are the ones who initially brought Reiki to the planet tens of thousands of years ago. They do not care if anyone believes this or not. This is just a piece of information that one can accept or reject. It does not matter to them what anyone believes about this. The last thing they want is for anyone to get into an argument over it. When there were enough Reiki Masters in spirit, Reiki was completely turned over to them, and The Ankenash stepped aside.

Getting back to permission-based systems, the BodyTalk System also requires that the practitioner get permission. The very first thing on their protocol is to get permission of the body, mind and spirit of the client. "Do I have all the necessary permissions?" is the first line of the BodyTalk System's protocol. They ask this silently, using muscle response technique, before asking anything else. If they cannot get permission via the techniques sanctioned by BodyTalk, they are taught not to work on the client.

Psych-K practitioners obtain permission as well. Before every single clearing they ask the client if it is "safe and appropriate" to do that clearing. They ask this by using muscle-testing. The "Is it safe and appropriate to balance for this goal at this time?" question is their form of getting permission.

Asking permission shows respect for the rights of the other person, and respect for her/his Soul's journey. It also demonstrates that you have healthy boundaries yourself.

Hopefully none of us would run up to a stranger and tell them they need an acupuncture treatment and jab a needle in their skin without asking first. Just so, we do not tell them if we see a dark patch in their aura which indicates impending illness of any kind. Nor do we give a "reading" that was not asked for, or do a healing that they do not know is being done. We use our skills when asked, or when permission is otherwise granted. This constitutes good boundaries. Planting a seed of belief about their health, such as impending liver disease, or their lives without asking for permission to do a healing or reading first is just egocentric nastiness. The Ankenash tell me that this will also incur negative karma for the intrusive reader or healer. Unfortunately this is a common error made by those new to the spiritual path in their eagerness to "help" others. My considered advice is simple. Heal yourself first. Then ask permission before doing healings or readings for others.

Chapter 8

The Ankenash Work on Me

After a few days of dictation in the wee hours of the morning The Ankenash found a way to get me physically ready for doing this work at a new level. If I were to speculate why they did it this way, the reason would be that I don't always trust what I am hearing. So for two weeks, every other night as soon as I would lie down in my bed to go to sleep, I would either get harsh indigestion or a powerful case of the hiccups. My solution for this was to go lie down on a special Koleai runner in my dining room. At first, I did this because I thought the flat hardwood surface under the rug would help me get the hiccups stopped. After lying there a few minutes I invited The Ankenash to come work on me. And they would arrive instantly. I could see, in my mind's eye, a version of them which was not the most recent one. They appeared as they had looked at an earlier stage of development, not as beams of blue light. I will describe them a bit later.

Gathering around me, they would vibrate and dance and sing wearing big floppy, round red hats. Half their bodies would be above my hardwood dining room floor, half would be downstairs, floating in mid-air. Everyone else in the condo complex was in bed by then, and the dining room was not near anyone else's bedroom. I believe The Ankenash wanted to work on me there instead of in my bed because the neighbors would not be affected, nor would their energy fields be close enough to affect mine.

While The Ankenash danced, bounced, bobbed around, vibrated and worked upon me, it seemed to me that percussive sounds were being made as well. After ten or fifteen minutes, my hiccups would stop or the indigestion would go away. Sometimes I would see them implanting something made of light into one of my chakras. The first night they came, it was my root chakra, two nights later, my second chakra. I could not tell clearly what those implants looked like, but I could definitely tell that this was indeed happening. Often I would be half asleep as they worked on me. I found myself feeling peaceful, much as I feel while getting a good massage from someone I trust without reservation so that I am able to truly relax to the point of surrender.

At some point during this time of being worked on every other night, I stumbled across a website for ayahuasca experiences in Brazil. Someone whose work I had admired for years, Stuart Wilde, was associated with them at the time. In this website, called *Heart of the Initiate,* were reports of experiences that were had by some of the participants in these sacred shamanic teacher-plant ceremonies. One such experience included Light Beings showing up to work on a few of the participants. These Light Beings were wearing large red floppy hats and bouncing and dancing as they worked on the participants. I noted the similarity to my experience; I believe The Ankenash were showing up in the ayahuasca ceremonies to assist with healing certain of the participants with whom they had prior relationships, maybe in this lifetime, or perhaps in another. I have also had other people email me after seeing the E.D.I.N.A. website that they are having blue beings show up in their healing rooms, too, but telling me that I was getting far greater detail than they were getting about how to do the healings. I appreciated hearing that The Ankenash were showing up in other healing rooms. The Ankenash told me when I asked that they know these healers and/or clients from other lifetimes or other versions of themselves in other frequential densities--or "parallel dimensions".

One morning after a dining room floor session with The Ankenash, I awoke and sat up in bed. I had slept later than usual and the sun was actually up. As I sat there, getting ready to stand up and walk to the bathroom, I saw something floating in front of my stomach which looked like a glowing fried egg made of light. The center "yolk" was a lovely, brilliant and intense ball of azo yellow-orange with a thin rim of turquoise light around it. What would have corresponded to the white of the egg was a creamy color with a few rings of bright light on the outer edges—perhaps violet-magenta and red-orange. I only saw this "egg" for a nanosecond, before it turned at an angle and slipped quickly into my upper abdomen. When it got inside me, I felt happy. Another morning during that time period I observed that there was some kind of large dark brownish, solid-looking, heavy geometric object located about eight inches below my feet on the mid-line of my Light Body. I only saw this for a nanosecond as well. I knew it was there to ground me, and that The Ankenash had placed it there. I did not yet know about the existence of the Earth Star chakra, but this is approximately where the object was located. I believe the reason that I saw these things at those particular times—upon waking and sometimes upon falling asleep—is because this is a normal human ability.

We are all of us more psychic the first few minutes upon awakening and upon falling to sleep. The psychiatric community even recognizes this phenomenon and calls these states of consciousness "hypnopompic" and "hypnogogic" states. These are simply times when we can all see into and experience the altered states of consciousness which are usually only available to the select few who are psychics, mediums and mystics—or to those participating in sacred teacher-plant medicine ceremonies. My own theory of the schizophrenic's delusions has to do with many schizophrenics becoming stuck in this in-between state, between sleep and wakefulness, wherein they cannot reclaim their ability see the same "reality" that the rest of us do. Paranoid schizophrenia is a completely different phenomenon, and should not even be called schizophrenia. It is most often caused by a demonic possession while the person remains lucid except for the paranoia and voices in most cases. But I digress.

I mentioned earlier that during this two week period, The Ankenash came to work on me exhibiting physical forms which were those of an earlier version of themselves. At differing points along the path to becoming multi-dimensional Starbeings, any given race of beings will have different developmental stages. For example, we know about ourselves that there are different versions along our developmental route: Australopithecus, homo erectus, homo sapiens and homo luminous beings. Homo luminous is where we are all headed. Beings on other planets have evolved from what we would identify as insects or fish or lizards and so on. Just so, The Ankenash did not evolve in precisely the same manner as we have; they evolved from birds. At one stage of their development, they had a torso, arms and legs as we do, but their heads did not have a nose and mouth. There was a beak in the same place where we have our mouths and noses. They did not have ears, but small openings in the side of their heads. And on their backs were large wings.

When I asked in meditation to see them up closer, they showed me a tiny section of their skin magnified and one eye. Their skin was a lovely blue-green, delicately wrinkled and iridescent-looking, like the skin around a bird's eye. This is the version of themselves they presented to me during the two weeks they prepared me to work on others using E.D.I.N.A. The predominant colors they were wearing were purple and red, including what looked like red capes and some very large, floppy red hats. There was a bit of gold as well. As they spread their wings wide, I could see bejeweled objects under the upper rim of the wings near their bodies. I could not tell what these gorgeous objects were, nor why they were there. I was only allowed to observe them. It was as if The Ankenash were showing them to me, but not explaining anything. At other times I would see them sporting solid gold helmets with a huge Mohawk-looking rim of red feathers fanning out along the mid-line. I could not see with the kind of detail I really wanted to see, but am grateful for having seen anything at all of this stage of their development. During our initial contact five years earlier, all I had been allowed to see were the tall skinny light beams.

I realized at some point after seeing this version of them that these beings must have been around me for a really long time, because I had been doing drawings, paintings and prints of "Bird Lady" in my twenties and thirties. She was often in Victorian era costume wearing a hat, pearls and long gown. I painted her with a "Bird Man" a couple of times. One line etching, "Bird Lady's Maiden Voyage" was reproduced in a widely-adopted college-level drawing text which Claudia, my major professor from graduate school in art at the University of North Texas, had written. The text was called, "Drawing: A Contemporary Approach," by Claudia Betti and Teal Sale. In this etching Bird Lady was flying in front of the house where my husband, children and I were living in Galveston at the time that I created the etching. I created quite a few more drawings and prints and paintings of Bird Lady. I thought she was just a figment of my imagination, however. Now I realize there must certainly have been some connection to The Ankenash. I am not saying that this is exactly what The Ankenash look like—just that I feel sure they must have been nearby or I would not have been drawn to create this strange image over and over in my artworks. I believe that while I was in my altered state of consciousness (or art trance) I could perceive them some-how. I suspect now that they have always been with me.

Chapter 9

The First Clients: the First Initiations

And so in 2007, after giving me the basic instructions, sending me supporting information in the form of books, websites, perhaps innocent comments from others, classes I stumbled upon by accident, and so on, The Ankenash dictated several sacred geometry forms. I was told one early morning to get out a compass and ruler, and standing over my dining room table in freehand on white smooth watercolor paper, I channeled these complex geometric forms. Later when I tried to reproduce them, I was completely, totally unable. The only way I could draw them again was on graph paper, and then with great difficulty. I was later to discover that their being on graph paper also meant that other people could absorb the images with both hemispheres of the brain in balance. I was told that some of these were initiatory symbols to be implanted in the initiates' chakras when I began to teach others how to invoke The Ankenash and to begin to practice E.D.I.N.A. themselves. The symbols were also to be used to meditate upon. If hung on the wall, The Ankenash have additionally said that the symbols will emit piezo-electric frequencies into the room for healing.

Next, I was instructed to begin working on clients using E.D.I.N.A.—asking them for feedback. I was told to work on female clients only at first, due to the complexity of the RNA/DNA differences between males and females. It seemed clear that The Ankenash were working out the details of the system as I worked on my clients. I was told that as soon as I had worked on five women, it would be time to work on the first male. They told me to ask the clients to report any "extra-dimensional effects" from the sessions. I was not sure what that meant, and thankfully my clients never asked what it meant. I was focusing on remaining in observer mode. And so I told one female client at a time what I was doing. I asked permission to invite The Ankenash into the healing room to work alongside me as I did my other forms of healing work. The Ankenash would be working in dimensions four through twelve as I worked using the other techniques I already knew. Each person I asked was happy to be part of this experiment, and I only asked clients I knew well.

When they returned for their next sessions, I asked about the extra-dimensional effects. The answer was always something along the lines of, "Well, I did not notice any extra-dimensional effects, but I did have my first out-of-body experience," or the first experience of a Light Being working on them as they awoke in the middle of the night, or the first experience of a lucid dream, or the experience of sudden, noticeable increase in synchronicity or in the ability to manifest with amazing immediacy, and so on. And then I realized was meant by "extra-dimensional effects." They were precisely what my clients had described was increasing in their lives. They were always eager for me to continue with "opening the E.D.I.N.A. portal" when I worked on them. We both felt the healing to be faster and more profound than with the other techniques used alone. Most could feel the presence of The Ankenash in the room. Then I began working on men. This went on for a couple of months, and then I was told announce the time and find a place to teach the first class in Basic E.D.I.N.A. I did that, and I wrote up a short instruction manual, based upon what The Ankenash had taught me, and had it printed. I was told precisely what date to teach this class, and only much later did I know what the date signified. It was August 15, 2007. This was almost to the day, the twentieth anniversary of the Harmonic Convergence in which my two young sons and I had participated at Enchanted Rock in Texas. It was also the anniversary of the ascension of Mother Mary. It was a profoundly significant date, but I did not know that at the time. I was just following instructions.

Thirteen people signed up for the first class. I was nervous; it was my first time to teach something I had "created" myself. Well, I had taken dictation and written the manual, at any rate. Some of the participants I knew very well and some I did not.

One was Margot, the new girlfriend of a long-standing, very spiritual male client of mine named Tom. I had seen her only a few times before as a client. I was surprised she was there. But she arrived over fifteen minutes late, after the class had already started, with an arrogant, dismissive air about her. This puzzled me. She stuck out like a sore thumb. Why was she there? Other participants in that class included several long-standing clients, many of them healers themselves, or perhaps good friends of mine who respected my work. The latter group was most excited to be a part of this first class of "E.D.I.N.A.: energy medicine for ascension." I had been told that this energy medicine was in its infancy and would need protecting initially. For one thing, that meant that the only time the students would say the word Ankenash in full was while invoking them. There was a rather long invocation sequence which involved the Overlighting Deva of Healing, Pan, The Ankenash, Healing Corps of the Ashtar Command from Sirius-B via the Spiritual Hierarchy, and the higher self or 8th chakra of the client being worked upon. So in common conversation, we were told to call The Ankenash simply

"The ANK" so as not to invoke them when they were not being called. A couple of years later I was told that it was okay
to say the name in full when we were given a shortened
version of the invocation sequence. It is interesting to note
that The Ankenash had told me at the time that the reason
humanity had been instructed "not to take the Lord's name
in vain" was so He would not be invoked when we were not
intending to do so. This made so much sense! Surely the
Godhead did not care if we said His name when angry. But it
made perfect sense that he had better things to do than to
respond when not being invoked...it was rather like getting
a wrong number or spam. You can hang up or delete the
spam, but your time and attention has been wasted already.
The more of this there is, the more time and attention is being wasted—time and attention that could be put to better
use. And the Universe deplores waste. This request of theirs
seemed imminently logical to all of us and we intended to
honor it fully.

I had also been told by The Ankenash of the importance of
taking monotomic elements** when we first began doing
E.D.I.N.A.. These build up and strengthen the Light Body in
the case of monatomic gold, and release dark energy that
we might pick up while doing the work in the case of monatomic black. It is actually with our own Light Bodies that we
do much of this work, so regularly feeding the Light Body is
important until we have been doing this work for a while.
Then we take them as instructed via our own inner guidance.

Another thing that was stressed was that I was to instruct
the students to listen to or watch The Ankenash for instruction about what to do next in the healing setting. The students were expected to be psychic/intuitive! I kept asking
if my students should use a pendulum or muscle testing to

determine what to do and in what order. The Ankenash replied that the students could use those in the beginning if they needed to do so, for confirmation. They added that it was most important for students/practitioners to begin to simply pay attention with their inner knowing, their claudience, clairsentience, claircognisence or clairvoyance and trust that. The Ankenash would be there to guide them, they had only to "listen and trust."

Recently in an advanced E.D.I.N.A. class, one relatively new student reported that she had been telepathically asking The Ankenash questions while working on her fellow student. The Ankenash wanted to know why she was asking all those questions when all she had to do was to trust, and be still and listen. They would tell her all she needed to know in the moment! It made me smile when she reported what they had said to her, since I had not told anyone that they had said this to me from the beginning.

I was also told that The Ankenash would not come into the healing room to participate even if the right words were said—if the person saying them had not been initiated. The initiation attunes the chakras so that the student can be quickly heard by The Ankenash, for one reason. Another reason for this was that they wanted practitioners to be properly educated about the ways in which they were willing to work with us. For instance, they are *not* willing to be our guardian angels or spirit guides. We already have those, and this was not The Ankenash's job; they did not agree to do this work at all. They did not want to be contacted to protect us, nor to give us advice, nor to answer questions. Protection is for the Guardian Angel(s) or Archangel Michael in dire circumstances; advice is the job of our Spirit Guides or our Higher Selves or other spirits who have agreed to do this type of work.

The Ankenash made it crystal clear that they were not available to do that kind of work. They were available to come into the healing room to work alongside us in the healing setting, but then only if we were the ones doing the healing. We were not to invite them in if we were the patient, or the one being worked upon. The reason for this was that if we were at the dentist, or the surgeon, or the massage therapist getting worked upon, that practitioner's own spiritual healing assistants would be present to help them do their work—whether they were aware of that or not. It was clearly a matter of protocol, and The Ankenash insisted in strictly following protocols. This was obvious that it was extremely important to them. I was much later to learn that Beings from Sirius had learned an extremely difficult lesson themselves regarding the importance of spiritual protocols a very long time ago, and had not forgotten this most profound and painful lesson. They had actually become the protocol masters for entrance into this Universe as a result of how well they had learned those lessons. If anyone at all wants to enter this Universe from any other, the protocol of our Universe is that they must go through a portal located at the triune star called Sirius to gain permission to enter for the first time.

That first initiation and class went well. I was quite pleased as were the participants. They practiced on each other after the initiations, and everyone seemed deeply impressed with the speed and efficiency of the work as well as the difference in the energy in the room as they called in The Ankenash and did this work for the first time. It was exciting for everyone, including me. I was extremely exhausted from doing thirteen initiations of seven chakras each, but felt really good about the entire experience. Oddly, the room I had rented for this first class, which was in the building where my office space was located, and had been vacant for several years was rented—the papers signed—during the precise time my class was being held. I wondered if it happened because of the Violet Flame Containment Field that we erected there and which remains there to this day, or perhaps because of the energy that The Ankenash brought into the space?

I started an online Yahoo Group Forum so that everyone could report what was happening and share experiences with each other. The online Forum was to be completely private. We were told not to share anything read on there with anyone who was not an E.D.I.N.A. initiate, so as to protect the privacy of the other people involved with this new and extremely unusual form of healing. However, now there is an open, public Google Group, and it is okay to use nicknames there. Some of the early initiates were psychotherapists who needed to talk about what was going on in their treatment rooms. Legally, these therapists need strict confidentiality in this matter. Others were people who needed the outer world not to know their names because they had jobs in which their job security might be threatened if anyone knew about their antics with something so strange as energy medicine brought to the planet via invisible blue people. We were also required to use our real names, not anonymous handles, because if we are being honest and open, so must everyone else, and so must they protect our anonymity in the outer world. Of course, if you felt the need to share something someone had posted and you got their permission to share it, naturally that was permissible.

**At this time, I order my monatomic elements at harmonicinnerprizes.com

Chapter 10

Early Experiences of the First Initiates

Many things happened after that first initiation. One of the first reports that I got came from Kelli, a massage therapist, who immediately began opening the E.D.I.N.A. portal the day following her initiation with every single one of her clients. She quickly became profoundly exhausted and after five days, she stopped opening the portal in order to give her body time to rest. Wisely, she had also ordered the monatomic elements, and after they arrived and she began taking them, she picked up a great deal of energy. Kelli began gingerly opening the portal again, but this time for just a few people a week until she built up her stamina for this work.

This was a valuable lesson for everyone. Part of this need for gentleness with ourselves was due to the fact that there were only fourteen of us in the entire world doing this kind of work at that point! The energy was very intense running through this small group. As the numbers grew, it got easier and easier for the individuals to do the work effortlessly, and the power of the work grew as well. The larger the morphogenetic field of any kind of energy medicine (the more people who do it) the more powerful it becomes for each individual, and at the same time, the easier it is on the individual healer's human form to actually do the work.

Early on one of the initiates asked me privately what steps to take to become a healer. Here is what I answered on the Yahoo Group (which later became a Google Group):

Someone has asked me privately what steps to take if they want to become a healer. I thought this might benefit everyone, so I will share my answer here on the group forum.

One of the first things to do is to begin to take classes to learn how to become a healer. Once you have been initiated into E.D.I.N.A., and taken the advanced classes when they are offered, Reiki is another good modality to add. A Reiki Initiation reinforces certain energy channels in the body. Everyone knows what Reiki is, or at least most people do, so that is an advantage.

It is not enough for a healer to have just one modality in my opinion. And as soon as you take each class, begin to practice so you get some experience in it. Let your internal guidance help you decide which classes to take and from whom. Listen to your own spirit rather than using logic. Pay attention to synchronistic events and to dreams. All healers will have their own "bag of tricks" so to speak. Each of us is different, and so what we are guided to learn as our unique set of modalities for our individual "toolbox" as healers will be slightly different.

And MEDITATE daily on a regular basis! Meditation is so important. This is how we build spiritual "muscle." This is how we learn to follow internal guidance, and to hear The Ankenash when they tell us what to do next in the healing setting. This helps in our own spiritual growth and improves our abilities as healers. The importance of regular meditation cannot be emphasized enough. Learn how to meditate properly. Meditation is not sitting quietly and thinking. When you are meditating properly you are not thinking. Sitting quietly thinking is called contemplation. Contemplation is not a bad thing, it is just not meditation. Meditation stills the mind.

Practice your healing arts on your friends and family with their permission. You will learn how to intuit which techniques to use in each situation, and your ability to hear your guides will have improved. After you have done this for a while, you will begin to get ready to charge money for the sessions. Each healer will have a different array of techniques, and combine them in different ways. The clients that are the right fit for each healer can then begin showing up.

When you are ready to set up a practice, it is a good time to take a marketing course. There are many good books on the subject, and various classes. You cannot sit in an office and just wait for people to show up. Well, you can, but you will be disappointed in the results. You do need to let people know you are there. And it is smart to start working out of your home to keep overhead low if that is at all feasible, and then when your practice builds you can rent an office because the size of the practice you have created will pay for it.

It is the rare new business that works well enough from the outset to support anyone, whether it is a restaurant, clothing store or healing practice. Most people either have a spouse who will support them while they are getting started, or cash reserves to live on while they build the practice. The third option is to have one foot in both worlds for a year or more. You can do your "day job" for years as you do your healing work part-time.

Hope that helps!

Hugs,

Lois

The one thing I would add to that now is that I believe that most people will always do this kind of healing part time. Indigenous shamans all have a "day job" and do healing work at night or weekends when someone gets sick—for which they are compensated. The reason that this works well is that this way no one is financially dependent upon people being ill, and at the same time, no one is taken advantage of as the healer is compensated. With energy medicine there must be an exchange of energy for it to work. It could be a chicken and some homegrown tomatoes, if that works for the healer. Money is concretized energy, and that is why it works as a medium of exchange for energy medicine. But a trade of goods or services keeps the energy flow healthy as well. The flow must go both ways for the energy medicine to continue to work, and for the healer not to become drained and useless as a healer. With family members, love is a medium of exchange, so long as the healer is careful to set good boundaries. It is important to know how to say "No," when we need to do that to take care of ourselves.

Hopefully, illness will become a thing of the past! I foresee a time when temporary imbalances can be handled by the patient (most of the time) and when that does not work then a healer can be consulted. At least, this is the vision I am holding for the future—and what I have seen when I peer into the future in a shamanic journey! There will be a few expert healers who are around to help out the neighborhood shaman/healer, or the seriously ill, and I suppose that they may do this work full time. I guess we will see.

Another of the initiates, Janie, reported this:

I just want to add my thanks to Lois for bring another wonderful class into being. I have not experienced any headaches or fatigue that has been mentioned in some of the other posts. I do feel a shift taking place—things that I have always enjoyed are now starting not to be important. I find myself thinking more and more about ascension, and what I

need to do to make the next step. That being said, I had one interesting thing happen. When I was meditating on Sunday (8-19-07) I saw a symbol that was carved into a large stone. The stone looked like sandstone, but I am not positive about that. It felt like the carving was very large. I am going to try and attach the picture I have drawn. I don't know if this has anything to do with the class or not, but I suspect that it does.
~ Janie

The drawing was of a sacred geometry symbol. Its significance might have just been for Janie, or it may be something of which we later realize the meaning.

Another E.D.I.N.A. initiate, Rae, reported that she had been experiencing a lot of synchronicities and did not relate that to E.D.I.N.A. until the morning of her post when she saw someone else's post about an increase in synchronicity. She stated that she felt a huge emotional shift in her life as well. Relationships were changing, too. Some were ending, others were deepening.

Dora, yet another initiate, reported to me that she had also been feeling extreme emotions. She was having trouble expressing them in writing. She felt irritation, but is a normally very easy-going person. Her dreams were very real and feelings during dreamtime were intense. She kept hearing someone calling her name at work and would turn around to see who it was calling, and find that there was no one there. She was encouraged that other initiates were having similar experiences with the odd occurrences, emotions, dreams and synchronicities. She did not feel so strange knowing she was not alone in this.

What I now would say about extreme emotions after having an initiation and/or energy medicine work done is that emotions are often felt again as we are healing and they are leaving our physical bodies—or being released. This is also how a homeopathic remedy works. To expedite this release of emotions I recommend apple cider vinegar baths. This will make the client feel better. There is no point in suffering needlessly.

I posted on the Forum after hearing similar stories from so many people that clearly E.D.I.N.A. is powerful stuff. I too had felt all these intense, overwhelming emotions while "taking dictation" from The Ankenash and bringing in this new form of energy medicine, but had no idea that was what was causing all of the emotions. (I mean—I was feeling joy, terror, and thinking "WHY ME?" and "I can't do this," plus feeling mild depression, etc.) I thought it was because I was getting BodyTalk from a new guy in Canada—at a distance. I had actually asked him to stop for a while.

But then after the first initiation Kelli was having the same "all over the place" emotions and so were several others, so perhaps for some people, this was part of getting used to the energies. I said I was not feeling like that any longer now that I was accustomed to the energies. So I had something to tell the next group of initiates, something to let them know this was temporary and was often a part of the initiatory process—at least it was in the beginning. And from several people's experiences it was clear that it was important to open the E.D.I.N.A. portal for themselves to be worked upon if they expected to do this kind of work on others. Later I realized that this intense emotional effect was just upon the first initiates, and gradually dissipated. It no longer happens when people get initiated. The early pioneers carried this burden.

Soon afterward Kelli emailed me:

Here is just a follow up on my email from last week. Today is the first day, that I have felt my energy coming back, a little more myself. To that end, I really wanted to use the E.D.I.N.A. today, even if it was just one session. So I pendled on it, and I got a cautious yes. When I connected I added the caveat that the energy only come through at a level that would not be difficult for me. The session went well and I disconnected immediately afterward. I then did several more massages and I only felt a twinge of the exhaustion that has plagued me the last five days. This evening I have been careful to eat well and rest, but even so, I have been informed that I have been more than a bit cranky. (Not sure if the full moon has anything to do with that or not). I intend to continue to con-nect for at least one session per day, building my muscle, so to speak. I have checked out the website for the monatomic element supplements that you recommended, and ordered the starter kit. I can't wait till it gets here.

I also want to second Janie's feeling that my feelings on ascension have greatly strengthened. My inter-ests are normally quite varied and I get a lot of pleasure from them. But recently I can't focus on those things so much. The prospect of ascension is really heady stuff! ~ Kelli

One person asked how much to charge for E.D.I.N.A., espe-cially for those who already have a practice, if we were to tack anything on extra price-wise for doing E.D.I.N.A.. Here is my answer:

This is entirely up to the individual, but I will share what I do. I use E.D.I.N.A. as an overlay to sessions and do not charge extra. Since I need client permission, the client knows why that session was different.

However, a straight E.D.I.N.A. session with crystals, Tibet-an bowls, etc. is charged at the regular rate of any of my other energy medicine sessions. The energy medicine ses-sion is what they are paying for, so I will not charge less or more for one type over another. (My Akashic Records/ past life readings and soul retrievals are different, so are not charged the same.)

I think whatever feels comfortable to you is what you should be doing, though. If you want to charge a bit extra to use E.D.I.N.A. as an overlay, then do that. Others please post about what you are doing if you are charging for E.D.I.N.A. at this time, if you feel comfortable about posting that.

I do not consider myself the last word on this topic at this point in time.
~ Lois

Further questions were asked about if you were a chiro-practor or acupuncturist, would it be okay to have the por-tals open in several places at one time if you have several clients in different rooms—and you were going back and forth between the rooms. The answer is that you leave the portals open, one for each client, while acupuncture nee-dles are in the client, whether you are there or not.

Another point which came up was the question of whether it were all right to open the E.D.I.N.A. portal for more than one person at a time, like a wife for herself and her husband lying in bed or meditating on the couch next to her. The an-swer was at first yes but for not more than two people at a time. Later it became all right to open the portal for up to five people at a time, for example in a group meditation. If there are two people opening the portal, then the group size can be twice as large, and so on. Clearly The Ankenash are gradually developing this system and expanding it!

The next obvious question was whether it would be okay

to open the portal for oneself and one's pet at the same time. The answer to that one is still no. The reason is that the RNA/DNA for the two species is so very different. It is permissible to do E.D.I.N.A. on animals, in fact we have learned a lot about the power of E.D.I.N.A. to heal serious illnesses from those who have worked on serious illnesses in their beloved pets. But we do not open the portal for two different species at the same time, like a human and a cat, or a bird and a dog. The Ankenash do encourage us to use E.D.I.N.A. on animals, in fact, because we love them so much, and because they are in the process of ascending as well in their own way. It is possible to use a wild animal as a surrogate for a larger group of the same kind of animals by asking permission of the animal group soul and the individual surrogate. We use a remote viewing (or distant healing) technique to get the required permissions in this case.

Other issues came up. At one point someone asked me, "What if a client reports feeling worse after a treatment?" That was an interesting question, but it has only come up once. Due to who it was that asked the question, I had two answers:

1. *If people report "feeling worse" after any energy medicine sessions, just remind them that "release work" after any energy medicine session can make the client briefly "feel worse" sometimes. When something comes up to be released we can feel it again briefly. This is true in homeopathy, and it is true with energy medicine. This temporary experience of "feeling slightly worse" briefly is an example of energy medicine working properly...when things come up to be released. However, this question also brings to mind a different answer as well.*

2. *Were drugs or alcohol present during the session?*

*Hopefully, one would never do E.D.I.N.A. or any oth-
er type of energy medicine, nor do any kind of spiritual work at all, not ever, while using alcohol or recreational drugs. This prohibition includes divination
as well. Nor would one use E.D.I.N.A. or do spiritual
work of any kind on a client who is under the influence of alcohol or recreational drugs. "Recreational drugs" includes street drugs like meth, crack and
heroin, as well as pharmaceuticals used recreationally. However it does not include the situation of
the shamanic ceremony which utilizes sacred teacher-plants.*

The term "spiritual work" includes (but is not limited to)
the use of a pendulum, Tarot cards, palmistry, rune stones,
or any other form of divination. Not doing this work while
high recreationally or drinking alcohol—this is for your own
protection. *It invites in dark energies* when you mix alco-
hol/recreational drugs with spiritual work. Again, this is not
true of shamanic experiences with *teacher-plants*, as long
as there is a true shaman leading the ceremony and invoking protection.

Unfortunately, there is a lot of confusion at this time in
Western culture about the difference between recreational
drugs and the so-called "drugs" used in the sacred ceremony in which shamans utilize teacher-plants. There is a growing body of research into the field of the kinds of altered
states of consciousness induced by various teacher-plants.
This movement is being spearheaded by people like Dan-
iel Pinchbeck, author of "Breaking Open the Head," which
chronicles which teacher plants take the participant where.
These plants have a conscious intention to teach and heal
humanity. Different plants take us to different distinct locations in non-ordinary reality, or space/time. This is what

Pinchbeck and the other psychonauts are researching on our behalf.

Teacher-plants are considered medicine by the indigenous people who have used them in religious ceremonies for centuries. There is nothing recreational about them. They are not fun. However, in the appropriate sacred setting, with a full complement of protective spirits invoked by the shaman, you are quite likely to have a profound, transcendent, healing experience at the level of body, mind or spirit or all of these. Some of these plants include peyote, ayahuasca, ibogaine, amanita muscaria, psylocibin, and salvia divinorum. And there are many more.

It is simply unsafe to utilize teacher-plants recreationally. And trust me—you just would not do it twice! A lot of the "bad trips" experienced by hippies in the 1960's were due to using some kind of drug or teacher-plant derivative, such as LSD, used in an unsafe environment, i.e. without a shaman invoking a circle of protection. The circle of protection keeps out any wandering dark spirits who might happen to be drawn to your increased light.

And speaking of dark energies, remember the person in the group who had arrived late for the first ever initiation, Margot? She reported something very strange soon after the initiation. She said she had gone to New York City to do her work as a filmmaker, and called in The Ankenash to protect her on those "dangerous streets." She said she felt very important and powerful having those five gigantic blue beings walking along beside her. She was asking them advice and guidance on a whole slew of issues and getting great answers, too. (At least that is where she thought the answers were coming from.) She also said she had gone to the chiropractor and opened the E.D.I.N.A. portal so The Ankenash could work on her at the same time. I thought that sounded odd, but did not quite put my finger on why. Puzzled, I got up from the computer and went into the living room where I had decided to paint the wall behind the television dark teal. I picked up the roller and continued with the work, switching to a large brush a few minutes later.

Having had many years' experience at channeling art, as I mentioned earlier, as soon as I started applying the paint with a brush I was wide open psychically. The Ankenash came into the room and made their presence known to me. They asked me what I was doing. I replied that I was painting. They then replied they were not talking about that, they then asked why I was allowing Margot to call them in to be her guardian angels and ask advice, and to open the portal when another healer was doing the work and she was not the healer, when they had clearly stated they were not available for that. It was even in the Basic E.D.I.N.A. Manual. I asked what I could do about it. They said to correct her now, in front of everyone, right on the Forum to put a stop to this kind of thing once and for all. I think my eyes must have gotten big. I stopped painting and asked if they were serious. They almost scolded me. They said it was my job to protect E.D.I.N.A. in its infancy, and that many forms of energy medicine over the past several thousand years had had to be abandoned due to pollution from the "dark side." They said they chose me in part because I am a fiercely protective mother, and that this "baby" now needed my fierce protection. I asked if Margot had something to do with the "dark side." They said that yes, she had a dark energy attachment. I wondered if I should give her the name of the person who removes those things, and they said I could offer to do that if I wanted to, but that I needed to stop painting immediately and go post a correction on the Forum. (Months later a psychologist and channel confirmed that one technique she practiced years prior had been shut down by its founder because according to the founder of that system, the system had been polluted by the darkness. I appreciated the confirmation.)

So I did stop painting the wall and go back to the computer to post on the Forum as The Ankenash asked. Without mentioning anyone by name, I reminded everyone not to open the portal if they were the client, only if they were the healer, and never to call on The Ankenash to act as security guards, guardian angels or advice-givers. And Margot went absolutely ballistic—right there on the Forum. Her vitriolic post was far beyond nasty. She wanted her money back for the class and initiation. I gave it to her. I also told her privately that I thought there might be a dark entity attached to her, and that I would be pleased to give her the name of someone who could remove it if she wanted. She vehemently denied the fact that there was a dark entity in her energy field or attached to her. I have since learned that when someone does that, they are not ready to let go of the entity. Maybe it makes them feel powerful. Or perhaps the lesson which the entity came to teach them was not yet learned. Most people if told there was possibly an entity attachment normally would say something like, "Gads, I don't think there is one, but if there is, I sure do want it gone!" I later learned that Margot already knew the name of the person I was then using to remove entities, and that it had once even been briefly removed by the lady, but came back in and reattached to Margot. The lady speculated that Margot needed the lesson still. Her belief was that the dark entities come to people to teach lessons, and that is how they evolve upward toward the light, and one way that humans can evolve as well.

Whatever the case with Margot, I let it go. I had done all I could for her, and she was on her own path with her own

Guides. Just like everyone else, her Soul was and is sovereign, and it was certainly not up to me to force a "fix" or healing upon her.

Early the next morning as I was meditating The Ankenash showed me a vision of Margot as seen from the back. I was not expecting this at all. In fact, I was taken aback with surprise. They then allowed me to see all seven of the initiatory symbols being pulled up and out through her crown chakra like pearls on a string. "Oh," I thought, "so that is how it works. They just pull them back out." Why did they do that? They did it because she did not want to get rid of the dark attachment. I wondered why this ever happened in the first place; why had she even shown up for my class at all? The Ankenash explained to me that the experience was allowed to occur in large part for my learning. What that meant became clear later, after I had a few more such experiences. The whole thing also happened to give Margot another opportunity to release the entity, and to grow and change, but she did not decide to take advantage of it. After her refusal to release the dark energy attachment, in order to protect E.D.I.N.A. energy medicine, the symbols were removed by The Ankenash. If she invoked them, they would not hear her. They did tell me if ever she later released the dark energy attachment, and wanted to be initiated again, that would be permissible and even welcomed.

Several times after that for a variety of reasons, that incident being the first, I have been accused of being too rigid, too strict, acting like a policeman, and so on. I felt badly when criticized, and I even doubted myself sometimes. But I knew with certainty that a "bitch" with a living child was better off than a "nice" mommy with a dead one. Sometimes when I doubted myself, I checked with The Ankenash, and they confirmed that I was definitely to protect

E.D.I.N.A. energies most fiercely in the beginning in spite of the disapproval of the "sweetness and light" brigade. They just did not understand my task and responsibility in the early days of E.D.I.N.A.! I lost a few people the first couple of years over my taking that firm stance, but was told that was a minor price to pay. Many of these people were not parents, or simply not very maternal or paternal, and did not understand. Or they believed that "ladies," which they mistook me for, should be nice all the time. But I am not a lady, nor do I aspire to be one. I am a natural matriarch and a female warrior, so my stance did not compute for them. I continued to protect E.D.I.N.A., my infant charge, in the face of criticism. I have since lightened up, but then, my baby is not a baby any longer!

Among the many things that The Ankenash told me in the early morning dictation sessions was this. They said that there would be 100 E.D.I.N.A. initiates within a year. I just rolled my eyes and said, "Yeah, sure." But actually, there were to my amazement, 100 E.D.I.N.A. initiates within ten months! Within two years, there were E.D.I.N.A. initiates on every continent except the north and south poles, just as The Ankenash also had said there would be. I was amazed.

These first initiates were certainly pioneers. They earned "gold stars" in their crowns as Souls, I suspect, by being among the First Hundred E.D.I.N.A. initiates. At least, that is what The Ankenash said to me. These are very special people, greatly to be honored. I am told that one day a huge marble memorial stone will be erected with their names etched in gold on its smooth face. The stone will be facing the rising sun, the place of new beginnings.

The next group to be assembled is the E.D.I.N.A. Core, or the first five hundred people. This will form the backbone of the E.D.I.N.A. energy medicine in the world, and allow it to spread and flourish into what The Ankenash tell me is a thousand years of spiritual healing in our world. They tell me I cannot imagine where this energy medicine is going, but that the roots are now firmly set, and the "tree" will soon begin to grow very large in our world, with thousands upon thousands of practitioners and instructors.

Chapter 11
Other Students with Entities

Briefly, I want to say that Margot was not the last student with an entity attachment. A few more showed up over the next year or so. I began to recognize them immediately, and when I finally did, they stopped showing up! This was yet another lesson which when I learned the lesson, I stopped getting that particular lesson. These folks all had similar characteristics, which I will share with you. Of course, please know that <u>not all disruptive students have entities</u>!

1. They all showed up at least 15-20 minutes late for class.

2. They always found a way to further disrupt class if I allowed them to join us.

3. They had a tendency to argue insistently with me, as the instructor, and behaved as if they were superior or more knowledgeable than I in some way—sometimes in every way possible.

4. They fought for the class' attention all the time, interrupting me.

5. They could cause me to become confused, foggy headed and/or exhausted if I made the mistake of looking into their eyes.

I finally quit allowing anyone to come into class who was more than fifteen minutes late. This took care of the problem. I also learned to tell anyone else who interrupted and argued with me that I was the instructor and they were not.

This clears the room of the anger and frustration that comes from the other students when someone is arguing and interrupting the instructor. It also quiets the student who is behaving inappropriately, whether or not they have an entity attachment.

Spirit teaches us like this. We are sent experiences to react to and learn from, and when we get the lesson, those types of experiences stop showing up in our lives. If we do not "get it" (learn the lesson) in this lifetime, the same lessons will show up in subsequent lifetimes via different scenarios until we finally do learn the lesson. This is the Earth School, and Souls incarnate here to learn lessons which are more easily permanently learned by that Soul while incarnated in physical form.

I also want to share this lesson I received about five years earlier than the incident with Margot. This happened when my metaphysical shop and bookstore, Hot Pink Lotus, was located on Huldy Street in Houston. It was slightly after hours one Saturday, and I was sitting on the floor with a traveling female shaman who was making the rounds selling her stunningly beautiful handmade feather fans and rattles. I was having a most pleasant time admiring her colorful handmade shamanic tools, trying to decide which pieces to buy for my shop. As we sat there, a customer came to the locked door who absolutely gave me the willies. She knocked insistently, and would not go away. Finally, I went to the door and told her we were closed. She was very pushy, and then found a compelling reason to come inside. I reluctantly let her in, but when she had bought what she said that she so desperately needed, I had a hard time getting rid of her. I did not know why she gave me the creeps, but she did. She was a clean, nice-looking woman with perfect manners. As soon as she was gone, Fran, the shaman, asked me why on earth I had looked into that woman's eyes. Did I not know that was how entities drain us of our energies?

I looked totally puzzled, I am sure, and she explained that this woman had a huge dark entity attached to her, and it was there in my shop that day to feed on my energy—which it had successfully done. I was shocked, and I was not sure I even believed in dark entities at that time, but it also deeply resonated. As I considered what she had said, I knew she was right; I was always exhausted after that woman was there. It even happened when she was in the shop, and I was in the closed treatment room and did not know she was there until I finished the session and came out! I did not know how to get rid of those entity attachments at the time. So the next time that the woman showed up, I told her she could not come in, nor could she come back until she found a way to get rid of the dark entity attached to her. I told her that I was unwilling to allow it to suck my energy any longer. I looked straight at her abdomen while speaking. She said not a word, turned and left, and I never, ever saw her again.

These days I actually do know how to get rid of entities, but I usually refer these clients to people whom I trust who specialize in entity removal. And the dark entities are no longer a problem in my classes. Looking back, I have come a long way from not even believing they existed just a few years ago to removing them or referring clients to people who do that.

Chapter 12

North Carolina – Sacred Geometry

The fall after I began initiating people I was guided to take a class in Ashville, North Carolina, about sacred geometry and healing. It was a four day long class. When I got there I realized that the class was, for the first two days, a review of things I had learned twenty years earlier at the Esoteric Philosophy Center in Houston. That first two days, I kept falling asleep because I was so bored. The second two days, however, I began to learn new material about healing and also about sacred geometry. In the case of healing, they were using tools: small LED lights—to introduce color into certain points on the body, usually meridian points, or so it seemed. They encouraged us to study further with a German man who had developed a technique for healing using colored lights. I thought this was interesting, since what The Ankenash had been teaching me was how to introduce specific colors of etheric light into specific locations on the body. This light was not in the visible range, however, and not generated by a machine. I wondered about the difference. I was taking all of this in, and did have an experience of partial healing from one instructor who was using the lights in specific points on my body.

I had begun feeling very ill with severe muscle cramps in my lower back immediately after I had said something at dinner the first night I was there—something which apparently upset a woman who had been there many times before. Without going into details, let me just say that I knew there was a cause-and-effect relationship. After the instructor used the colored lights on me, I felt about 75 percent better. It was a major relief, and as a result, I knew from experience this method worked.

The woman I had angered was named Janetta. I deduced later that she had used one of the techniques that this particular school in Asheville taught people to use for healing remotely. But she used it to harm me, because as soon as she left on the last day, I instantly felt completely well. I know she was not actually taught how to do evil with the technique, but I also know she had somehow done that. Doubtless she had racked up some seriously negative karma for herself on that trip. Misusing healing techniques to harm another person is a very bad idea. It is the equivalent of black magic. The damage done comes back to the "evil-doer" many, many times over. The sad thing was she did this to herself just to get even for something I said which she did not like. This is an indicator of major ego involvement, just so you know and can identify the same in yourself, should you ever get seriously upset about someone disagreeing with you in a conversation over dinner.

Yet so many good things came of that trip that I am still very glad I went. They were just not what I was expecting. I was expecting profound knowledge of sacred geometry techniques that I could use immediately, and I was expecting a deeper understanding of the sacred geometry symbols that The Ankenash had given to me. Instead I learned to respect and even be wary of misusing sacred geometry, even accidentally. I learned what part of the dome and the pyramid to avoid sitting under, and how to slightly alter the shape of a pyramid or dome to make it safe to sit anywhere under it, among other things.

I also learned something new about the safe use of a pendulum. Certain shapes are profoundly powerful, and must be used with caution. These are not often found easily, and

I have never seen one in metaphysical bookstores, so please do not be concerned. Additionally, I learned that you become what you pendle. For example, if you spend a lot of time pendling to diagnose or locate cancer, you are likely to develop cancer. I learned that if you use certain specific sacred geometry forms in a precise way, you can do great damage to yourself as did one prominent radiesthetist in the '30s in France. So I learned what not to do. The information on pendling in this class comes directly from the experiences of the French Radiethesists in the 1930s.

An additional treat on this trip was that I met four amazing, loving and kind women, a group of friends from California who were psychologists. I realized after having dinner with them one night that I needed an emotional support system, and that I did not have one. I told them over dinner about The Ankenash and about E.D.I.N.A. They did not for a moment doubt one word of it, and in fact, were very supportive. The one who had spontaneously invited me to have dinner with them had actually seen The Ankenash once before—about fifteen years earlier in her garden very late one starry night. She was all alone at the time. Frightened by their size and sudden appearance she had asked them to leave, and they did leave. They have respected her request and never have come back. Another of these women, Connie, loaned me a book the next day, which contained one of the most important things to come out of the entire experience in Asheville. She followed inner guidance in offering it to me. I am grateful.

In this book Connie gave me I read something that put my mind to rest, even though it was just a tiny piece of my mind with a nagging question hiding deep in a remote recess. The question was how to know with absolute certainty who is speaking to you when you get information telepathically. I knew people would ask me this eventually. I was not sure how to answer.

What I learned was that there basically three types of Beings to be aware of and to know about. First there are the really heavy-duty, badass dark entities. They have a name, but I do not want it in this book. We all know about them and that they do evil in a profound way. We do not need to be concerned with them further than this brief mention.

There are however, two types of Light Beings, and it is the difference between them that is important to our discussion here. First, there are the Luciferics. Yes, Luciferics are actually of the light, but they do not understand what we are doing here, and they do not truly have our best interest at heart. They think that being on a planet which is a school and involves pain is just pointless. Luciferics simply do not understand about the Earth School, or that we are here by our sovereign Soul's choice prior to incarnating on Earth, to learn and grow through our experiences and from the consequences of our decisions while on Earth. It is just not in their frame of reference at all. And so they do things to distract us. Many unfortunate people have followed them, much to their Soul's ultimate detriment. What they do is tell us how amazing and great we are, and pump up our egos. Luciferics cannot be bothered with confirmation of anything they tell you in the outer world. It is too much trouble. Profoundly lazy, they become elusive or tricky if you ask them who they are and where they came from. They will not give their names nor tell you from where they originated.

Now, why do we want to avoid beings who pump up our egos? If you are desirous of spiritual growth, a pumped up ego is the last thing you need *if you are an adult with an already healthy ego.* The ego is here for the mundane things; to drive the car, balance the check book, change the diapers and so on. Spirit is here to make the big decisions such as choice of career, marriage partner, parenthood and the like. Where ego is concerned, mature adults are different than children. Children are in the process of building their egos so they can function in the world, so they do not need to have them crushed. They need their self-esteem built up so they have a strong, functioning ego. A healthy ego is necessary to function properly in the world. Only a healthy ego can get out of the way to allow for spiritual growth, which is why getting emotionally healthy is a piece of the spiritual path at some point for spiritual seekers.

The other type of Light Being is the kind we want to work with if we are interested in spiritual growth, which is, after all, the whole purpose of being on Earth in the first place. They include Angels, Archoi, Archangels, Ascended Masters, Chohans, Starbeings and the like. These beings will aways tell you their names and where they come from immediately—just as soon as you ask or even wonder. They will give confirmation in the three dimensions, or in the outer world, of everything that they tell you. It is not ever too much trouble for them. And they will never, ever, pump up your ego, though they may reassure you if you have doubts about yourself. This perfectly describes The Ankenash, and I was greatly relieved to be reminded of this information. I had learned it initially at the Esoteric Philosophy Center more than twenty years earlier, but had forgotten. If this were all I had gotten from going to North Carolina it would have been worth it, but it was not, as I have already mentioned. I learned a lot more.

Part of the "more" that I learned had to do with the nature of how to use light. The Ankenash had previously told me that we were using a special kind of etheric light, one that is created/invoked by our consciousness, because it was of higher quality than anything generated by machines. When I saw people using LED lights, I wondered why am I being told not to use that instead? It seemed far easier. The question of using machine-generated light versus etheric light like The Ankenash were showing me was a question for which I would receive an answer later. I was to learn that it was an extremely important question. It had to do with the Fall of Humanity, and it had to do with our future as a race of beings. We humans are evolving into a new type of being called not angels, but "Spirits of Love and Freedom." Why? Love because it was out of love we chose to evolve in the direction toward Source. Freedom because we were the first experiment in which beings were given free-will and still made that choice to move toward our Creator. We were given freedom and chose well out of love!

Chapter 13
The Fall of Humanity

So let us now talk about "The Fall," in an attempt to understand what that was all about. It was a fall in consciousness. We were once far greater beings than we are today, far beyond our ability to imagine at this time. This Fall has been talked about in many ways in various texts over the past many thousands of years, and it is all the same basic story though told from different and varying perspectives.

Tellis Papastavros tells this story in his book "The Gnosis and the Law." I will give a very abbreviated version of that here. Earth was clicking along at a nice pace, with human beings ascending at regular intervals. Things were going smoothly. We were an ideal planet for spiritual growth and eventual ascension. Due to our continued successes, over hundreds of thousands of years, our spiritual hierarchy kindly decided to host beings which had not been at a level appropriate for ascension when their own worlds had ascended. These unfortunate beings then had nowhere to turn to continue their spiritual evolution. They were floating aimlessly in space, so to speak. So we let them in. However, when these beings came in, as the door was opened, some very dark beings got in. They have since created ongoing havoc on our planet, including creating all the predatory animals! Because of these dark beings the ascension process has been stalled for everyone for hundreds of thousands of years. Were it not for the loving intervention of a very powerful being of light called Sanat Kumara, we would have been destroyed totally to put an end to this horrific darkness which had infected us. Instead, we were just "shut down" so that we became three-dimensional beings, unaware of our twelve dimensional potentials. This was done to protect the rest of the Universe from our horrific infection—and give us time so that we might have a chance to heal. This is a differently worded version of what is also reported by others, such as Bob Frissell, in whose books I read it first, and also by his teacher, Drunvalo Melchizedek.

They tell essentially the same story, but from a quite different perspective. Here is my abbreviated understanding of their version. At a time when Atlantis was still above the water and functioning properly, the people who lived on Mars had pretty much destroyed their own planet. They did this by focusing on the development of external technology, like machines, instead of spiritual technology like energy medicine, or meditation-induced states of superior consciousness, healthy merkabas, and ultimately ascension from which eventually flowed eternal life. Higher consciousness is a part of spiritual technology. When any race of beings focuses on intellectual development over their spiritual/consciousness development—or the mind over the heart—they get into trouble. They cease to feel. They lose compassion for others and the planet. Usually they eventually destroy their planet. When the Martians did destroy their planet's ability to support life, the last of them came here. They created an external merkaba to get here—not the internally generated, spiritual kind since they were preoccupied with external technology. They then created for themselves a colony on the southeast coast of what is now the United States—approximately at the location we now refer to as North Carolina.

Several hundred years later, a comet or meteor or some such heavenly body was headed for Earth. The Atlanteans wanted to leave it alone, since such things are natural since they come from the Creator or the Source of All That Is. The Martians had the notion that the celestial body aimed at us should be shot out of the heavens before it hit. There were more Atlanteans than Martians, so the Atlantean view prevailed. However, when the heavenly body hit right in the midst of the Martian colony, the Martians decided it was time to leave Earth.

They attempted to construct an external merkaba again, but no one could really remember just how to do it properly. After all, it had been many hundreds of years since their ancestors had come to Earth. None of them were still around. When they constructed the faulty external merkaba, they created a rift in the space/time continuum which allowed a hole in our protective field. This allowed horrific dark beings to come to Earth and attack humanity. This was the beginning of what is referred to as the Fall of Humanity. There is much more to this story and if you are interested, read Frissell or Drunvalo or Papastavros. Oh, and in case you are wondering, most of that darkness is gone now; the rest will be gone soon. Not only living people but spirit beings have been busy sending these dark ones to their own version of heaven where they can continue to evolve, eventually returning to the Light. They simply do not belong here. But that is a huge subject for a different book.

The only reason I mention this story at all is that it is the question came up for me in North Carolina at the class in November of 2007 as to the difference between using the etheric light in the manner which the Ankenash were teaching me, and the LED or electrical lights used by the man in Europe and his students here in America. As I said, their technique actually works. The Ankenash wanted me to know early on that this form of light working for healing existed. At the same time (take note, as this is important) they wanted me to know that the reason we were to use etheric light was of huge importance to our future as a race of beings, because it supports the growth of our own internal, spiritual technology! This is something we will need to be able to take with us as we evolve into higher functioning spiritual beings!

It was within weeks after this class in North Carolina that I picked up the first book I had ever seen which had been written by Bob Frissell, "Nothing in This Book is True, But It's Exactly How Things Are." It led me to Drunvalo's work later. Ten years earlier I had been curious about Drunvalo's work, but my Guides steered me firmly away from him. I now realize that this was so that what he had been told would act as a confirmation of what The Ankenash would tell me years later! They wanted me to understand why using machines when we can do something with our own spiritual abilities is a huge mistake. Look at what it did to the Martians. It destroyed their planet, and eventually damaged ours. If they had been meditating and developing spiritually (working from the level of the heart not the head) instead of solely focused on external technology at the expense of spiritual technology, they would have been able to create their own individual internal merkabas and travel through space at will. There would have been no destroyed planet Mars, and consequently no damage would have been done to our planet nor to our ascension cycle.

To summarize, even though mechanical lights can work in a limited way to heal us, in the long run the human race is better off using etheric light in the manner being taught by these twelve-density beings, The Ankenash, because doing that kind of work helps us to evolve spiritually, rather than devolve the way the Martians did. Developing spiritual technology is eminently good for us!

Chapter 14

The E.D.I.N.A. Tree Grows

The Ankenash are telling me that the first four years after I did the first initiations and classes acted as the seedling stage for E.D.I.N.A.. They now tell me that the root system of this tree, metaphorically speaking, is ready to grow into a massive, large tree. It took four years to get there. And now it is time for me to take E.D.I.N.A. to the next level. This level includes making public how to do Basic E.D.I.N.A. Considering the way in which E.D.I.N.A. was begun, the incredible care taken to protect it in its babyhood, I am beyond amazed that The Ankenash are telling me I am now to give openly the instructions about how to do Basic E.D.I.N.A., and how people can initiate each other without my involvement or that of any instructor. If this seems too complicated after you have read it, and you prefer to pay an instructor or me to do your initiation, of course we will. The Initiations can be done at a distance. Just go to the E.D.I.N.A. website http://www.edinahealingtemple.com, and contact any one of us listed on the instructor's page with an asterisk before our names. We can do the initiations at a distance.

However, if you want to initiate a friend and have them initiate you, then you may after you read the instructions given here carefully. The Ankenash give their permission for that, so long as you do not charge money. (If you wish to charge for this service, you must become a Certified E.DI.N.A. Instructor—see website for how to do that.)

First I will tell you the core information about Basic E.D.I.N.A. This comes from the Basic E.D.I.N.A. manual, and is material has not yet been covered in this book. It is highly recommended you read this book in its entirety before you attempt to do initiate anyone or do E.D.I.N.A.

I want to make very clear that The Ankenash will definitely communicate with you in the healing setting once you are initiated. They may speak to you like a voice in your head. Or they will give you instructions via a felt sense, a knowing, or visual images in your mind's eye. These are instructions given for the individual client/situation. They are not meant to be new techniques for advanced classes, or taught to your students as part of Basic E.D.I.N.A. or any advanced classes. If you think you are getting new techniques for advanced classes, contact me, Lois J. Wetzel, and tell me what these are—I will ask The Ankenash about them. If these techniques are incorporated into advanced classes, you will be acknowledged and honored for your contribution to E.D.I.N.A.. The Ankenash have made it quite clear that at this time, I, Lois J Wetzel, am the only person who is their agent for this method on Earth. This is for the purpose of continuity and to avoid confusion. When that changes, I will be told.

Before we go any farther, I must remind everyone that it is not safe to do E.D.I.N.A. or any other form of energy medicine or spiritual work including divination while under the influence of alcohol or recreational drugs, or while your client is under the influence. This prohibiiton includes pharmaceutical drugs used recreationally. This prohibition is for your safety and of those around you. Dark energies are attracted to alcohol and recreational drugs used in a spiritual environment. Again, this does not apply to proper shamanic rituals utilizing teacher plants.

Meditations &
Practicing E.D.I.N.A.

Before doing E.D.I.N.A., the initial action to take is that you want to do two separate meditations. The first meditation you will do is to create a clean, safe space in which to work, and into which The Ankenash can enter. This is called the violet flame containment field meditation. You will be creating a field of energy that will remain permanently in that space for the purpose of transmutation of the darkness to the light. After you create it, check periodically to see if it is there if you wish. It usually remains there unless there is a major disturbance to the space, such as an earthquake, hurricane, bombing, tornado, tsunami, and so on.

The Violet Flame Meditation

The meditation is quite simple. You only need to do this once for any given location, not every time you do a healing session. Sit quietly with your eyes closed in the space you wish to fill with the violet flame. The violet flame is for purification of a space. Imagine a carpet of tiny violet flames covering the floor of the space. If there is an open doorway or window, imagine a sheet of glass or plexiglass covering that to hold the shape of the space which the flames fill. In your mind's eye, watch the field of violet flames slowly fill the room, rising gradually upward like water filling a swimming pool. Gradually it will rise up and up until it has filled the space. You can do this anywhere you like, in an office, a home, a public place like a church, grocery store or bank. Unlike E.D.I.N.A. or Reiki, BodyTalk, Matrix Energetics, and so on, the use of the violet flame is not permission-based.

When we utilize the violet flame, we contribute to the increase of the light quotient on Earth. This is an important contribution to the evolution of humanity as a whole. So if you were to go about erecting violet flame containment fields everywhere, this would be a good thing!

The violet flame is held in consciousness on behalf of humanity by St. Germaine, one of the Ascended Masters and a member of the Spiritual Hierarchy of the Earth. You can find out a great deal more about the violet flame on the internet. There is a plethora of information there.

Now here is the second meditation. This second meditation, the Qui Gong Meditation, is highly recommended for you to do daily for your own personal growth, but especially it is important that you do this before doing an E.D.I.N.A. healing session. This method is a powerful yet simple way to connect to Source, where all the healing energy comes from in the first place—it is in fact where everything comes from. Source is also sometimes referred to as the Unified Field, or as the Zero Point Field in scientific circles.

The Qui Gong Meditation:

1. Imagine that you are standing on the Earth, or you can actually stand. Now see a smile of thick warm oil melt all the way down the front of your body from the top of your head down to the bottoms of your feet. Take your time.

2. Imagine that a smile of thick warm oil melts all the way down the back of your body from the top of your head to the bottoms of your feet.

3. Imagine that a smile of thick warm oil melts all the way down the inside of your body starting at

the top of your head to the bottoms of your feet.

4. The energy of your feet melts down into the earth all the way to twice your height.

5. You imagine that are now a large tree with roots into the earth and energy now comes up the roots into your body.

6. Bring that light into the central channel of your body which runs from root chakra to crown chakra like a big tube.

7. The light you have brought into your body is alive. Feel its aliveness.

8. This light becomes thick like gelatin.

9. Now bring the energy down from the cosmos above you into the central channel at the crown of your head.

10. Open your pores and bring in positive environmental energies.

11. The light in your central channel expands into the trunk and shines brightly, then expands back out of all your pores into your aura.

12. You are now ready to begin your day or your healing session, filled with Source energy.

This next meditation is optional, and can be used to increase your psychic and healing abilities if you so choose. It can be done occasionally or daily—your choice. Close your eyes before beginning any of these meditations. Meditation increases our spiritual qualities/abilities. It is "spiritual weight-lifting."

Balancing the Third Eye:

1. Imagine a glowing golden ball of light floating before your forehead. As you inhale sharply through the nose, feel that the energy/light is being drawn in through the Third Eye to the center of your head. It brings in warmth and radiance to the clairvoyant center of the mind. Exhale gently, leaving that golden light in your brain. Repeat four more times.

2. Imagine a ball of silver light at the back of your head where the head joins the neck. As you inhale sharply through your nose, feel that energy being draw in through the foramen magnum (or the dent where the skull meets spine) to the center of your head to mix with the golden light. Repeat four more times.

3. Sit quietly, feeling at one with the Cosmos.

How to work on your client using E.D.I.N.A.:

Once you have been initiated, and your client is on the table and you have permission to work with them, you are ready to begin. If you do not think your client will agree to being worked upon by blue people from Sirius-B, find a way to word getting permission that is acceptable. Language is important. There are many ways to word your question that will not be frightening for your client. For example, I might say, "Do I have your permission to connect to an energy field that is more powerful than mine, in order to facilitate your healing?" Or I might ask, "May I open the E.D.I.N.A. portal so that I am able to work with super-powerful energies to maximize this healing session for you?" or "I work with a healing field of energy more powerful than my own, and I am going to connect with that now if it is okay with you." If you are relaxed about getting permission, you will. If you act nervous and dodgy, the client may feel reluctant to go ahead.

Before working on the client, open the E.D.I.N.A. portal. You can say it aloud, or subvocally. In the beginning everyone had to say the following to open that portal:

1.   I now connect to the Overlighting Deva of Healing.

2.   I now connect to PAN.

3.   I now connect via the Spiritual Hierarchy to The Ankenash, Healing Corps of the Ashtar Command. (Corps is pronounced CORE.)

4.   I now connect to (insert name of person being worked on)'s Higher Self/8th Chakra.

After you have said the fourth line, then **open the vortex** with your hand pointed at the floor as described in detail below. *Please do not forget this step. This drains off the pathogenic energies or detritus released by the client during the session; and you do not want that gunk getting on you or anyone else in the immediate environment. It would be rather like walking around in a sewer. (More on this later.)*

Once you have the above memorized, so you know what the open E.D.I.N.A. portal actually means, you can use the shortcut. "I now open the E.D.I.N.A. portal," instead of saying the four steps listed above. It is important to memorize it so that when you do E.D.I.N.A. years from now and someone says, "How do you know what you are connecting to?" you will know absolutely the answer to that question.

And why do we connect to the Devas called the Overlighting Deva of Healing and PAN? We connect to them because they are the male and female devas who created all life on Earth. Creator/Source created the O.L.D. and PAN first, of course, and instructed them to the task. For that reason we honor them just like we honor any other members of the Spiritual Hierarchy. Yes, the Devic Kingdom is actually part of the Spiritual Hierarchy. For those who have studied MAP healing, The Ankenash borrowed the connecting method from them because the morphogenic field was strong and they/we were given permission from the Spiritual Hierarchy to "piggy-back" on it in the beginning to align E.D.I.N.A. initiates and their clients with The Ankenash.

Immediately after opening the E.D.I.N.A. portal, you will create a vortex in the floor to carry off pathogenic energies which will be released from the client as you do the session. Do this by pointing at the floor and making a clockwise circle if you are on the side of the planet where water drains in a clockwise direction when you drain a sink, like in the USA. However, if water drains counterclockwise as it does in Australia, then you will make the vortex counter clockwise (or anti-clockwise as the Aussies say). If you are in a location upstairs doing this work, visualize that the vortex drain snakes between your floor and the ceiling below until it gets to an outer wall and then goes down the side of the building until it hits the ground. Once there, the pathogenic energies will be transformed into positive energy for the light bodies of plants/trees...like energetic fertilizer! We do not want the vortex to drain straight down if we are upstairs, because we do not want the detritus, or pathogenic energies, to contaminate any lifeforms inhabiting the space below us.

Once you have opened the portal, you are ready to begin your healing session. You can use E.D.I.N.A. as an overlay to other modalities, and The Ankenash will simply work on your client in the expanded realms as you do your other modality or technique. Or you can do straight E.D.I.N.A. Remember, E.D.I.N.A. energy comes through your hands like Reiki once you are initiated. If you already do Reiki, then after you are initiated, E.D.I.N.A. will come through like an upgrade to the operating system in your computer. You can open the portal and simply lay your hands on your client. That is quite enough. If you want to get fancy, there is more you can do. Some specific techniques which are precisely E.D.I.N.A. techniques are to follow.

First of all is the main technique called "Drawing Down the Light," instructions below. Drawing down the light is the primary Basic E.D.I.N.A. technique beyond laying hands on the client. It is simple to do, and the majority of "recipients" can actually feel it when you do it. This still amazes me. Something I create with my intention, and draw down into the client with my imagination can be felt by most of my clients! Even if it cannot be felt by some, they normally can see the results of the sessions in their lives, unless they are especially resistant to self-observation or self-reflection.

When you finish your session you will say, "I now close the E.D.I.N.A. portal." Even if you are opening your session with the long version, you can still say, "I now close the E.D.I.N.A. portal," when finished with your session. If you forget to close the portal, both you and your client may become quite tired. If you realize later on that you forgot, or you even think you might have forgotten to close the portal, just close the portal when you realize this, even if several hours have passed.

CAUTION: When your client is relaxed and being worked upon, there should be no sudden movements or loud noises. Be quiet and gentle so as to not shock them in this vulnerable state. Thoughtlessly doing this can fracture the

*client's aura and allow energy loss from the various shells
of the aura, as well as make them vulnerable to "dark"
or intrusive things getting inside their auric fields that do
not belong there. Either of these could harm them. This is
important; they trusted you as a practitioner to protect and
care for them by giving you permission to work on them.
Please remember that doing this work is an honor.*

Instructions for Drawing Down the Light:

When we draw down the light, we close our eyes to increase
our ability to focus. The client is on the table or healing surface. You can use a dining room table with a thick blanket on
it or a pallet on the floor if you do not have a massage table.
The portal has already been opened, and we listen to the
Ankenash with our eyes closed. Sometimes we hear words
in our heads, or see an image of what they want us to do, or
just have a felt sense. If you need to check what you think
they want you to do with muscle testing or with a pendulum, go ahead. They say this is okay as you are just starting,
but they want you to focus on just listening to them and
doing what you hear/see/feel needs to be done. Trust yourself to get instructions from The Ankenash, but at the same
time, do not make something up because you are in a hurry
to "do something." Be patient, close your eyes, and listen/
sense/watch.

So, what to do when you do get instructions? If you are instructed to draw down light into the liver, you will see from
the next list called "concordances" of the Chinese Five Elements that the proper color to go into the liver is green.
*(Later on you will see a link to my illustrations of all of this
including locations of the major organs in the body.)* So up in
the air at about the level of your head, but directly over the
client's liver, with your eyes closed, form a ball of pure green
light with your intention. Form this ball using your hands.
Take your time. The ball should be slightly smaller than a

basketball. Once you feel/intuit it is solidly formed, draw down a stream of light from that ball straight down into your client's liver. Draw down this beam of light until you can sense that the liver is filled with light. At the same time that you are drawing down the light, pathogentic energies will be released from your client, and fall through the table into the vortex below. The vortex will move around to catch the energies on its own, you will not have to think about it or direct it. The pathogenic energies will be drained out of the space via the vortex you created when you opened the portal. At the end of the session when you close the portal, the vortex will close all by itself when it has finished draining out the released pathogenics. It will close all by itself just like a vortex of water draining from your sink disappears when the water is all drained out.

Here is a word about the vortex. If there are pets or small children in the healing space, which there should actually not be while you are working, they will be drawn to the vortex. I do not know why, but I have seen it happen over and over. They do not need to be standing in that vortex anymore than they need to stand in the toilet bowl while you flush the toilet. Pets and children in the healing setting are most distracting anyway, and for that reason should not be present while you are working on someone. If you are working on yourself and want to open the portal for yourself and your child, that is good. If you want to open the portal to work on your pet separate from people, this is a good thing, too. But if you are working on someone else, it is a good idea to be free of other responsibilities or distractions. Your attention and complete focus should be on the healing that you are doing.

Again, on the page below with Concordances you will see which colors go into which organs. In the advanced classes, this becomes more complicated and there are much more detailed techniques, such as what color goes into each of the major muscles, the meridians, the central nervous system, the dantiens, the extraordinary vessels, as well as how to remove dark energies, disease extraction, temporarily removing the Lightbody from the physical to extract objects stuck there from past lives (like a sword you died from) and still causing problems, and more. We learn how to use sound in the healings as well, and we work with the Hathors of Venus for that work—all in the Advanced E.D.I.N.A. classes.

If you still your mind, open your heart, and just listen and trust while you are connected to E.D.I.N.A. energy, The Ankenash, who have been invoked when an Initiate has opened the portal, will speak with you about what to do next. Do not try to figure it out logically. Energy medicine works at a level that is beyond what the conscious mind can comprehend, so logic is "out the window" so to speak, and so for the most part, it is rather useless.

Remember, you must be initiated before The Ankenash will hear you invoke them and come into the healing room and work with you. They set it up this way so that they would not be casually invoked just because someone was talking about them. Instructions on how to initiate someone follow in the next chapter of this book. If you do not feel you can do it, you are welcome to contact me or one of my instructors to initiate you at a distance.

Concordances for Drawing Down the Light

We will be working with drawing down the following colors light to work in specific areas. There are five colors: green, red, yellow, blue, and white (same as the Chinese Five Elements/Medical Chi Gong). Each color corresponds with one of the five elements. Listed below are the colors, elements and some of the concordances.

Wood Element
Bright Green Light

Organs: Liver & Gall Bladder

Emotion: Anger Consciousness: Soul

Fluid: Tears

...

Fire Element
Intense Red Light

Organs: Heart & Small Intestine

Emotion: Joy/Sadness

Consciousness: Spirit

Fluid: Sweat

...

Earth Element
Bright Lemon Yellow Light

Organs: Pancreas, Spleen, Stomach

Emotion: Worry

Consciousness: Essence

Fluid: Saliva

...

Metal Element
Pure, Bright White Light

Organs: Lungs & Large Intestine

Emotion: Grief

Consciousness: Animal Instinct

Fluid: Mucous

...

Water Element
Deep Velvety Midnight Blue Light

Organs: Kidneys, Bladder and Reproductive Organs

Emotion: Fear

Consciousness: Willpower

Fluid: Urine

...

Special Notes About Color:

You will notice that *we have not indicated a use for orange etheric light.* This is because it must be used with caution. It must never, ever be used in the heart, brain or eyes, as it can cause damage. We are not talking about ordinary orange-colored light, but about orange etheric light, the kind you create with your intention/imagination. The only time orange is used is when it is drawn down into a blood clot or tumor that you want to break up, and only if you know precisely where that tumor or clot is located. Conversely, blue is opposite orange on the color wheel. That is what you use if you want to get bleeding to stop, as it will cause blood to clot! Draw down blue light into a bleeding wound to help it stop bleeding. (Also apply pressure, of course, and cold packs if you have them.)

Purple or violet etheric light can be used in the brain but not anywhere else.

White light can be used anywhere and everywhere. White light is what you use when you do not know what color goes into any given location. It is safe to use white light anywhere in the body. The body can then extract the frequencies from the white light which it needs at that location in the body, because white light is the combination of all the colors of light in the entire spectrum. Additionally, you can use it because The Ankenash tell me that it is safe to use everywhere.

Possible Side-Effects from E.D.I.N.A. Energy Medicine:

Besides the initial reported effects of lucid dreaming, out-of-body experiences, increased intuition, more synchronicity, more vivid dreaming, more immediate manifestation, clearer guidance from one's angels or guides, and Light Beings coming to you while you are asleep or meditating and working on you, there are other things that can happen simply as the result of any form of energy medicine.

Emotional, career, and/or life situation changes are as much possibilities as are physical healings when we are getting E.D.I.N.A. sessions. Some clients come in for a painful knee joint or headaches and see other things heal first, because the body's innate healing wisdom prioritizes. It knows what lies beneath the symptom that is bothering you and addresses that first. Perhaps the client gets a new job out of the blue or their marital discord is healed, or the kids or pets start to behave, and so on...before the knee gets better. Maybe the headaches quit after the chronic back pain they thought they had to live with forever gets cleared up. Or the knee quits hurting after the constipation they've suffered with since childhood goes away. There are things that our conscious mind does not yet understand, but the innate healing wisdom of our body absolutely does understand.

Anything that our bodies or minds can do might happen after a session as the body is balancing itself. These may include temporary, unusual changes to the urination, bowel movements, sweating, rashes, itching, brief skin breakouts, mild muscle soreness, and/or vivid dreaming. Tiredness and increased thirst are the most common reactions and they usually occur the first day, so drink plenty of water and rest. The most common report we get is that peace and joy are the result of getting regular E.D.I.N.A. sessions!

Doing E.D.I.N.A. on Yourself

You can do E.D.I.N.A. on yourself daily by opening the portal while you are lying down or while meditating and lightly placing your hands on your body. The E.D.I.N.A. energy flows through you and to the place in your body where it most needs to go. It comes in throught the crown chakra down the central channel (pranic tube) to the heart. There is bifurcates and goes down the arms and travels to the hands where it enters your body. This light will be directed to wherever it needs to go all by itself. The Ankenash will see to that. So just relax and let it happen. You do not need to do anything else; just surrender as the Ankenash work on you in the densities one through twelve.

Twenty to thirty minutes at a time is what is recommended for self-treatment. (It is not recommended that you fall asleep for the night while leaving the portal open. If you think you might, just sit up in the bed rather than lying down.)

If the client is on medication, the need for meds may increase briefly and then decrease dramatically as the body is balancing itself, so high blood pressure and those with insulin dependent diabetes would need to be monitored carefully. *All clients need to be told this.*

Apple Cider Vinegar Baths

Emotional releases could occur after an E.D.I.N.A. session, and for that we suggest apple cider vinegar baths. This will release the emotion into the aura where it can subsequently be showered out of the aura. To a very warm bath add two cups of apple cider vinegar and soak for thirty minutes, then drain the tub and shower fully. My clients have been using this bath successfully for over twenty years. All report that they sleep very deeply after taking one of these baths. It is important *not to add anything else to the bath besides the apple cider vinegar.* Please add your special salts and oils to a different bath on a different night, as the vinegar will not work the same way if you add other chemistry to the mix.

Chapter 15

Doing E.D.I.N.A. Initiations

This chapter contains the instructions on how to initiate someone into E.D.I.N.A. energy medicine. You and a friend can do this for each other. If after reading this you do not feel that you can do this, contact me, Lois Wetzel, and you will be scheduled with either Lois or one of her instructors who can do remote initiations for your E.D.I.N.A. initiation, if there is not an instructor near you. For this service you will need to pay the amount listed on the website. You can do this for free yourself, though, if you study the following instructions and follow them carefully. Readers of this book can initiate others for free, but they may not charge for initiations. If anyone wants to charge for the initiations, he/she is asked to become certified to become an E.D.I.N.A. Instructor. Check on the E.D.I.N.A. website if you are curious as to who is allowed to charge a fee for the E.D.I.N.A. initiations. All are listed and the ones who can initiate remotely have a red asterisk before their names.

Special Preparation Notes:

Before you begin, place copies of the seven E.D.I.N.A. sacred geometry forms on the wall or somewhere that you can easily see them. If you are already a Reiki Master, you will probably be familiar with the following technique, since it is similar. Tell your students before starting, that each time you tap their shoulders gently they are to raise their hands in prayer position above their heads.

To see the E.D.I.N.A. sacred geometry forms and a few other helpful E.D.I.N.A. images/illustrations go here: https://picasaweb.google.com/loisjeanette/BasicEDINAImages

You have my permission to print them for your private use. For any commercial use at all, you will need permission from me, Lois J. Wetzel, in writing. They are copyrighted.

If the following initiation sequence seems complicated, that is because it is. You will want to practice a few times on a teddy bear or large ball, or something like that. This will not seem complicated if you are a Reiki Master already.

Procedure for Initiating Someone into E.D.I.N.A.

This is a step-by-step guide to doing an E.D.I.N.A. Initiation. If there is more than one student, have the students sit in a row of chairs, sitting side by side. Before starting the meditation/guided visual journey, tell them that when you put your hands on their shoulders, this is a signal that they are to raise their hands in prayer position above their heads. Show them what that looks like. Stand in front of them and put your hands in prayer position just slightly above your head. Of course, their eyes should be closed as soon as you begin the meditation, or they will not be going anywhere in the meditation. Standing behind your seated student(s), lead them into a light trance by taking them on a guided visual journey. If you are not comfortable creating a guided visual journey, you can read aloud the one that follows this description for initiating someone into E.D.I.N.A. Once you have taken them to a place where they can sit/pause in the journey, you will:

1. Close your Governor Channel:

(Place the tip of your tongue behind the front of your upper two front teeth. Keep it there until you have completely finished the initiation. At the same time, you will clench your kegel muscles* and keep them closed until you have completely and entirely finished the initiation. If you open the governor channel, you must start over from the beginning, so keep it closed.)

2. Still standing behind your student, create a vortex with your hands a couple of inches above their head. Your left hand is on the bottom, face up, and your right hand is on top, facing down. You will hold the left hand stationary, and make counterclockwise circles with the right hand. This opens an energy vortex.

3. Look at the symbols. One at a time, you will blow the symbols into your student's crown and then their hands. You will blow around your tongue, the tip of which is still touching the gumline right behind your two front teeth. The first symbol you will visualize and blow into the top of the student's head is the vesica pisces inside a sphere, which is two overlapping circles. Visualize that symbol (in three dimensions if you can) and blow it into the crown chakra.

4. Gently tap/touch their shoulders and they will raise their hands in prayer position above their heads. Then you will blow the vesica pisces into their hands at the thumbs. After you have done that, gently push their hands back downward. This one is for the crown chakra.

5. Repeat steps two through four again, but second time, you will blow in the ten pointed star to the crown and then the hands – for the brow chakra.

6. You will repeat the above sequence a total of seven times, once for each symbol.

7. The next sacred geometry form you will blow in is the six pointed star – throat chakra.

8. The square with the small circle inside is the next one to be implanted – heart chakra.

9. Then next symbol to blow in is the one with three circles, a triangle and cross – third chakra.

10. The next symbol is the eight pointed star. (two squares at 90 degree angles) – second chakra.

11. The last symbol is the Julia set – root chakra.

12. Finally, to seal the symbols in, blow the square with the dotted line through it into the crown chakra, but not the hands. The square rotates counterclockwise if viewed from above, with the dotted line as its axis.

NOTE: The sacred geometry forms are three-dimensional. Visualize them that way if you can. If you cannot do not worry, The Ankenash will take care of it.

<u>Now you can release/open your governor channel!</u>

If you are initiating a group of students, you will keep the governor channel closed the entire time. Again, you will be behind them the whole time you are initiating; their eyes are closed. Blow the first symbol into each student's crown and hands and then move down the row to the next student. You will implant the first symbol into each student before returning to the first student in line. Then take them into and altered state via the guided visual meditation. Then blow the second symbol in, and then go on down the row to each student in turn implanting that symbol. You will do this with each symbol until all symbols and the final seal have been implanted.

After you have completely finished the initiations, you help your student(s) to return in the guided journey the same way they went in, retracing their steps exactly. When they are back to the spot of origin, tell them to very gently begin to wiggle their fingers and toes and then gradually open their eyes. It is important to come back slowly and gently from the journey. Many students become deeply relaxed and go into a powerful altered state of consciousness, and it is important not to surprise anyone in this vulnerable state.

*Kegel muscles: To learn how to close these you will need to practice interrupting your urination. While you are urinating, if you stop mid-stream, you have closed the kegel muscles. Practice stopping and then starting urination again. This is the way one can learn to gain control of the kegels and become familiar with closing and opening them.

A Sample Guided Meditation for the Initiation Sequence

Use a relaxed and peaceful, gentle soft tone of voice at all times when guiding any meditation. Ask your students to close their eyes and get comfortable, removing any tight or binding belts or ties. Make sure you have all taken a bathroom break before starting the meditation/initiation sequence. Everyone's comfort is important, so ask if the room is too hot or cold, or if they need anything to be more comfortable. Softly playing instrumental music, like "new age" or piano or violin in the background is helpful, so long as it does not contain any sudden changes or loud surprises. It is your responsibility to protect your students so they can feel relaxed and safe the entire time. The room needs to be semi-darkened if possible; turn off the lights and lower the shades. Make sure no pets or small children or any other distractions are present. No one who is not involved in the meditation/initiation should be coming into the room. All phones should be turned off. Make sure there will be no sudden, loud noises, as those can be harmful to someone in a deep meditative state. Now you can begin the meditation.

Tell the students that some people visualize more easily than others, and if they cannot visualize, ask them not to worry, just to listen to the words and relax. Read the meditation <u>slowly</u> in a quiet, relaxed, peaceful monotone. Close your own eyes, and see the scene in your own minds' eye once you get this meditation memorized. It is okay if you make changes as time goes on and make it your own. Here it is:

"Imagine that you are safely walking barefoot down a sunlit path through the woods. It is peaceful and safe there. There are birds and butterflies, and playful squirrels dart joyfully among the trees. The earth is soft underfoot and the air is comfortably warm. There are flowering bushes along the side of the path giving off a delightful fragrance. Occasionally in the distance you see deer grazing peacefully on the undergrowth. The path winds softly through the trees, finally veering around a curve to the right where you see an open meadow. You leave the path to walk across this meadow.

The grass is cool under your feet. You can see small yellow flowers growing among the blades of grass. As you walk across the meadow you see a temple. There are stairs leading up to the entrance to the temple, and a row of large glowing angels with gleaming swords made of light guard the entrance. As you approach, they raise their swords and cross them high up in the air so you can walk underneath, as a sign of respect and protection of you as you walk up the stairs. The temple door swings open widely all by itself as you approach.

Walking inside the temple, you see that inside it is one

large room with a beautiful chair in the center. The chair is there for you. This chair stands in the middle of a large circle of water-filled golden bowls with one large pale white lotus floating in each bowl. Each lotus glows brightly with a flame that does not burn it up. The flame is coming up out of the center of each flower. You step carefully through the circle, move to the chair, and sit down. As you do, spirits may come into the room. Perhaps these are loved ones who have passed over to the other side, angels, spirit guides or simply orbs or energy forms who are here to honor you at this sacred time of spiritual initiation."

Now the initiator stops talking and does the initiation sequence, silently blowing in the symbols as described above. No talking should occur at this time at all. When finished with the initiation, having blown in all seven symbols to crown and hands of your client, finishing with the "seal", you may opt to allow your students a few moments to speak with the beings in the room. Softly tell them this. Then after two or three minutes, continue the meditation. Still using a soft, quiet monotone, tell your students it is time to say good bye to the angels and other Beings who came to witness the initiation. Take your time, and guide the students back out of the circle of bowls, across the temple and back out the temple door, down the stairs past the angel guards. Then crossing the meadow, guide your student(s) back up the path through the trees to the point of origin in the meditation where they will stop. When you reach that point of origin, tell them to begin wiggling their fingers and toes, and gently begin to open their eyes. Give them a few minutes to do this comfortably.

Next you may wish to ask them if there is anything they would like to share from the experience of the initiation—such as spirits seen, and so on. Explain that this is entirely optional and some classes/students will share quite emo-tionally and freely, some have nothing to say at all as it is very private to them. In other classes, a few students will share while others will not. Take care not to imply any judg-ment about this. It is up to each student if he/she wants to share this extremely private, sacred moment with others.

Of course, after you have done this meditation a few times you may wish to change it up or create one of your own. Many times students will tell you after a guided visual med-itation that they saw what you told them to see, but they saw it right before you said it. This is normal. This happens because you are actually entering another reality together. It is called the Imaginal Realm. These are very *real* places, in non-ordinary reality—but it is a shared reality nonetheless.

If you do not want to lead the meditation yourself at first, you can go to the website and play the one that I have recorded. http://edinahealingtemple.com/default.aspx?menu-itemid=242

This particular page is not listed on the website; it is a spe-cial link just for people who have read this book.

Next, give your students a chance to practice doing E.D.I.N.A. upon one another. Watch them carefully, correcting any er-rors as they occur. It is easier to learn it correctly the first time, than to unlearn an incorrect methodology. Remind them that if they are connecting to the "Overlighting of Deva of Healing" for example, using the long version, then it must be said exactly that way. Once a student of mine de-cided she preferred "The Goddess of Healing." Fortunately I heard her and corrected her immediately. It is not okay to change this method. That would be disrespectful to The Ankenash, who will then decline to work with that person, because they are not taking the method seriously. The student does not know better than The Ankenash which words to use to open the portal.

Especially do not let your students forget to open the vortex in the floor to release/drain out pathogenic energies. If they do, those energies are all over the floor like a black cloud, and can contaminate the energy fields of others coming into that space, including the healer and his/her family and pets. You would not walk around in fecal matter, so why would you walk around in the energetic equivalent?

It is important to observe your students when they first begin to practice. If there are too many to do that, have the students break into groups of three to practice, with one person holding the manual** or this book and acting as the coach. They then will take turns being the healer or coach or client. You will still move from group to group to listen for a while and offer support or answer questions as they come up.

At the end, have your students assemble for closing so they can share or ask questions. If you do not know the answer to the question, please do not try to make something up. Tell them you will find out the answer and get back to them. Go back and re-read this book if you do not know the answer or check the older posts on the "Open E.D.I.N.A. Google Group." Encourage students to join the E.D.I.N.A. Google group. Even more on E.D.I.N.A. is there. This is where we ask and answer questions about Basic E.D.I.N.A.

Your students are now ready to practice E.D.I.N.A. on their friends, family and pets. If you or any of your students decide that you are interested in Advanced E.D.I.N.A., please direct them to the E.D.I.N.A. website, where one can sign up to take the classes as distance study—to be done at your own pace. These classes are far more advanced and time-consuming than Basic E.D.I.N.A. More teaching is involved and quite a few more techniques are given. In person the advanced classes are two-day classes. So the student will want to become rather familiar with E.D.I.N.A. by having done Basic E.D.I.N.A. on themselves and a few clients/friends/family/self or pets before taking an advanced class. Most people do at least fifty sessions before taking advanced classes.

** A Basic EDINA Manual can be ordered here:

http://www.edinahealingtemple.com/default.aspx?menu-itemid=243

It will come as a PDF file and you can print the full Basic E.D.I.N.A. Manual out from that file.

If you decide that you want to study Advanced E.D.I.N.A., contact me, Lois Wetzel, via the E.D.I.N.A. website. These classes can be taken at a distance for self-study. Check the website periodically to see who I allow in the future to teach these advanced classes in person.

E.D.I.N.A. First Hundred

These are the first one hundred people to be initiated into E.D.I.N.A. energy medicine. They are to be honored always for assisting this form of energy medicine come to exist on Earth by allowing their bodies to be among the first to carry the frequency. I bless and thank them from the depths of my heart, each and every one!

E.D.I.N.A. Core

These are the first five hundred people on Earth to be initiated into E.D.I.N.A. energy medicine. As of this writing in 2012, we are still in the process building the E.D.I.N.A.

Core. So if you want to be part of that special group of people in history, now is the time to be initiated into E.D.I.N.A. Because of the very important nature of this work, we are keeping up with who these people are. If you and a friend initiate each other, please contact *edinaenergymedicine@ gmail.com* and tell us your name, address, email and phone number. We will not be bothering you in any way, but if you are a member of the E.D.I.N.A. Core, or even an E.D.I.N.A. Initiate at all, we want to know that you exist. If you decide to initiate more people, please do notify us as to who they are.

Conclusion

As I close, I wish to say that it is my fondest hope that E.D.I.N.A. Energy Medicine for Ascension will sweep the planet so that The Ankenash may assist with the ascension of humanity as is so much their fond desire. I pray that you will answer the call if you are feeling guided to assist with this ascension of humanity and the Earth herself, and with your own spiritual growth by participating in E.D.I.N.A. Energy Medicine from the Stars!

While initially I did not want to do this at all, bringing E.D.I.N.A. to the planet, having thought I had already been asked to do enough risky, strange, bizarre, off-the-beaten-path things in my life, I am glad I did. So many people have already benefited, and I am sure there are those who will benefit in the future. I have not been even slightly comfortable in this scary process; it took a lot of courage. By sticking my neck out like this, risking being called insane or worse, I have discovered something important. It is this: courage is not at all the absence of fear. Courage is feeling the fear and doing it anyway.

It has become clear to me that part of my calling is to do what my Soul wants done in this lifetime, not what my personality/ego feels comfortable doing. It is also one of my tasks to "demonstrate courage" so that others may follow my example, reasoning that if I can do it, so can they. This was a lovely confirmation which I recently got from Dr. Peebles, channeled by the sweet Summer Bacon right on my BlogTalk Radio Show of February 10, 2012. So I hope you will take courage from my exploits. This would make me smile!

The Ankenash, Healing Corps of the Ashtar Command of Sirius-B, wish to express their appreciation and gratitude. They so love working with us. They are our progenitors, and they adore us beyond anything we can imagine. They say we may be able to imagine this depth of love after we have "arisen from the ocean and are finally floating in the air" alongside them. They can see the future, and they already see us there.

LUMINOUS BLESSINGS!

Lois J Wetzel,

Founder of EDINA Energy Medicine

E.D.I.N.A. Energy Medicine from the Stars

www.edinahealingtemple.com

edinahealingtemple@gmail.com

Other books by Lois Wetzel:

Akashic Records: Case Studies of Past Lives

Sacred Journeys and Vision Quests

References/Links:

To order a Basic EDINA Manual:

http://www.edinahealingtemple.com/default.aspx?menu-itemid=243

Initiation Meditation-Recording:

http://edinahealingtemple.com/default.aspx?menu-itemid=242

EDINA Images/Illustrations:

https://picasaweb.google.com/loisjeanette/BasicEDINAImages

EDINA Website: EDINAhealingtemple.com

Lois' website: Hot Pink Lotus.com

Lois' Radio Show: BlogTalkRadio.com/lois-wetzel Lois Wetzel's show airs at 9 am Central Time on Fridays (except when she is travelling) at the time of this writing. Listen free in the archives anytime.

EDINA Google Group: Just go to groups.google.com and type EDINA Open Group in the search engine on that page. Anyone can join!

Notes:

Lightning Source UK Ltd.
Milton Keynes UK
UKHW011913150522
403039UK00001B/8